Entrepreneurial Finance at the Dawn of Industry 4.0

Entrepreneurial Finance at the Dawn of Industry 4.0

Editor

Quan-Hoang Vuong

MDPI • Basel • Beijing • Wuhan • Barcelona • Belgrade • Manchester • Tokyo • Cluj • Tianjin

Editor
Quan-Hoang Vuong
Phenikaa University
Vietnam

Editorial Office
MDPI
St. Alban-Anlage 66
4052 Basel, Switzerland

This is a reprint of articles from the Special Issue published online in the open access journal *Journal of Risk and Financial Management* (ISSN 1911-8074) (available at: https://www.mdpi.com/journal/jrfm/special_issues/Entrepreneurial_Finance).

For citation purposes, cite each article independently as indicated on the article page online and as indicated below:

LastName, A.A.; LastName, B.B.; LastName, C.C. Article Title. *Journal Name* **Year**, *Article Number*, Page Range.

ISBN 978-3-03943-597-5 (Hbk)
ISBN 978-3-03943-598-2 (PDF)

© 2020 by the authors. Articles in this book are Open Access and distributed under the Creative Commons Attribution (CC BY) license, which allows users to download, copy and build upon published articles, as long as the author and publisher are properly credited, which ensures maximum dissemination and a wider impact of our publications.

The book as a whole is distributed by MDPI under the terms and conditions of the Creative Commons license CC BY-NC-ND.

Contents

About the Editor . . . . **vii**

Preface to "Entrepreneurial Finance at the Dawn of Industry 4.0" . . . . **ix**

Quan-Hoang Vuong
An Unprecedented Time for Entrepreneurial Finance upon the Arrival of Industry 4.0
Reprinted from: *J. Risk Financial Manag.* **2020**, *13*, 224, doi:10.3390/jrfm13100224 . . . . **1**

Thanh-Hang Pham, Manh-Toan Ho, Thu-Trang Vuong, Manh-Cuong Nguyen and Quan-Hoang Vuong
Entrepreneurial Finance: Insights from English Language Training Market in Vietnam
Reprinted from: *J. Risk Financial Manag.* **2020**, *13*, 96, doi:10.3390/jrfm13050096 . . . . **5**

Viktoriia Koilo
Evidence of the Environmental Kuznets Curve: Unleashing the Opportunity of Industry 4.0 in Emerging Economies
Reprinted from: *J. Risk Financial Manag.* **2019**, *12*, 122, doi:10.3390/jrfm12030122 . . . . **29**

Hong-Hai Ho, Thi-Hanh Vu, Ngoc-Tien Dao, Manh-Tung Ho and Quan-Hoang Vuong
When the Poor Buy the Rich: New Evidence on Wealth Effects of Cross-Border Acquisitions
Reprinted from: *J. Risk Financial Manag.* **2019**, *12*, 102, doi:10.3390/jrfm12020102 . . . . **47**

Dzung Phan Tran Trung and Hung Pham Quang
Adaptive Market Hypothesis: Evidence from the Vietnamese Stock Market
Reprinted from: *J. Risk Financial Manag.* **2019**, *12*, 81, doi:10.3390/jrfm12020081 . . . . **63**

Thi-Hanh Vu, Van-Duy Nguyen, Manh-Tung Ho and Quan-Hoang Vuong
Determinants of Vietnamese Listed Firm Performance: Competition, Wage, CEO, Firm Size, Age, and International Trade
Reprinted from: *J. Risk Financial Manag.* **2019**, *12*, 62, doi:10.3390/jrfm12020062 . . . . **79**

About the Editor

Quan-Hoang Vuong (Ph.D.) has been the Founding Director of the Centre for Interdisciplinary Social Research at Phenikaa University in Hanoi, Vietnam since 2017, and has served as Senior Researcher at the Centre Emile Bernheim de Recherche Interdisciplinaire en Gestion (CEBRIG), Université Libre de Bruxelles, Belgium since 2003. He has (co)authored over 150 journal articles, book chapters, and books, including ones in the world's leading journals such as *Nature, Nature Human Behaviour, Scientific Data, International Journal of Intercultural Relations, Studies in Higher Education,* and *Palgrave Communications,* to name just a few. He is also the Lead Editor of the book *The Vietnamese Social Sciences at a Fork in the Road* published by De Gruyter, Sciendo imprint in 2019.

Editorial

An Unprecedented Time for Entrepreneurial Finance upon the Arrival of Industry 4.0

Quan-Hoang Vuong [1,2]

[1] Center for Interdisciplinary Social Research, Phenikaa University, Yen Nghia, Ha Dong District, Hanoi 100803, Vietnam; hoang.vuongquan@phenikaa-uni.edu.vn or qvuong@ulb.ac.be
[2] Centre Emile Bernheim, Université Libre de Bruxelles, 50 Ave. F. D. Roosevelt, 1050 Brussels, Belgium

Received: 23 September 2020; Accepted: 24 September 2020; Published: 25 September 2020

Abstract: Enterprises and entrepreneurs in emerging economies face a different set of opportunities and challenges from the fourth industrial revolution, Industry 4.0. This volume comprises a number of analyses on entrepreneurial finance with a focus on the emerging markets, covering topics such as debt financing, stock market efficiency, resource consumption, and sustainable development.

Keywords: entrepreneurial finance; emerging markets; Industry 4.0; sustainable development

---

The world today abounds with examples of technological advancements that have generated both opportunities and challenges. The Special Issue "Entrepreneurial Finance at the Dawn of Industry 4.0" of the *Journal of Risk and Financial Management* brings attention to a number of finance topics that are often under-researched in the discussion of Industry 4.0 and its impacts on entrepreneurship. In particular, the issue seeks to better understand entrepreneurial finance in the context of emerging economies where automation and globalization present different risks (Vuong 2018).

Besides corporate finance, the volume considers how entrepreneurial opportunities in Industry 4.0 could re-shape the education and environment of emerging markets. Risk assessment and management in such settings, as the authors have noted, requires paying attention to the cyclical patterns of market inefficiency and corrections, the external equity financing, the consumption and import of resources, and even the potential disruption to existing models due to technologies. In re-evaluating assumptions and old beliefs, the authors have also pointed out that cross-border mergers and acquisitions (CBMAs) do not always have a positive effect on shareholders' welfare in the long run, a finding that diverges from the literature and carries weight in long-term financial planning.

In terms of financial management, the authors included in this issue have examined the sources of firm financing, the financial determinants of firm performance, the trends of cross-border mergers and acquisitions (CBMAs), and the sustainability basis for economic growth. Entrepreneurial debt financing is shown to take different forms, ranging from traditional sources, such as bank loans, venture capital funds, angel investors, and corporate investors, to informal sources, such as loans from family and friends. A study on fluctuations in stock market returns also sheds light on elements affecting financial markets, which in turn may help in predicting financial crises and market crashes.

The articles vary not only in terms of topic discussion but also in their methodologies. First, the use of data, which covers the periods both before and after the dawn of the new technological revolution, provides insights into the kinds of changes that are transforming society and the market. Second, the authors have utilized a variety of models, including the environmental Kuznets curve hypothesis, the adaptive market hypothesis, the propensity score matching (PSM) model, and the differences-in-differences (DIDs) model, in addition to applying frequentist statistics and conducting group interviews and thematic analyses.

In a study on entrepreneurial finance in the English language training market (ELTM), Pham et al. (2020) present empirical evidence for the financing sources of start-ups in this market. The authors show that global edtech start-ups have attracted a three-fold increase in investment in merely one year, from US$55 million in 2018 to US$150 million in 2019. Consistent with this trend, in the particular cultural setting of Vietnam (Vuong et al. 2020), the ELTM is one of the most lucrative segments. The prevailing view among the studied subject is that the growth of this market has been turbo-charged by technologies that are emblematic of Industry 4.0: mobile apps, online platforms, and social networking sites such as Facebook and YouTube. In contrast, the financing mechanism of such start-up efforts in the ELTM is very traditional; entrepreneurs rely mainly on private sources such as family and friends.

Similar to the ELTM, cross-border mergers and acquisitions (CBMA) have also reached a new level of growth since the arrival of Industry 4.0. Ho et al. (2019) explore the wealth effects of CBMA from emerging to developed markets, describing the phenomenon as "when the poor buy the rich." The authors consistently estimate the negative effects of such deals in three-, four-, and five-year event windows, which could potentially reach up to −69% after five years. The non-cash financing method is also shown to have a strong negative wealth effect after three and five years. Such results highlight the complexity of the CBMA and serve to discourage business owners from emerging economies from considering their future M & A in advanced markets.

To understand the wave of companies from emerging markets looking to buy others in developed markets, it is necessary to roll back a little and study how companies from the less developed markets are doing. Here, Vu et al. (2019) shed light on the determinants of enterprise performance through an analysis of nearly 700 firms listed on the Vietnamese stock markets. The authors find that capital intensity is negatively correlated with firm performance. For financial firms, there is a negative association between performance indicators and the age of a firm and average wage per employee. The evidence suggests there is still a high level of reliance on low labor cost and labor-intensive and low-tech production among Vietnamese businesses.

In a different approach to entrepreneurial finance, Koilo (2019) zooms out at the macroeconomic picture to find signs of sustainable development. Using the annual data on GDP, the net inflows of FDI, energy intensity, and the trade openness of 11 emerging economies in Eastern Europe and Central Asia, the author studies the relationship between economic growth and environmental degradation, measured as carbon dioxide (or CO_2) emissions. The findings not only affirm our understanding of a carbon emission Kuznets curve for these emerging economies, but also cast doubt on the differential impacts of the information and communication technology (ICT) sector on the environment; the usage of new technologies is correlated with increased energy consumption, and, subsequently, higher CO_2 emissions. In the wake of Industry 4.0, such empirical pieces of evidence suggest that more investigations are needed to draw any link between technological applications and CO_2 emissions. In the meantime, as part of financial risk assessment and prevention, policies aimed at introducing and developing new technologies in emerging economies should be evaluated carefully before being put into practice.

Lastly, any inquiries into entrepreneurial financing would be amiss without taking into account the stock market and the dynamics of private equity returns. While the stock markets in emerging economies such as Vietnam remain small in scale and trading volume, understanding their behavior prior to the applications of more advanced technologies is of critical importance. In this volume, Tran Trung and Quang (2019) test the adaptive market hypothesis, which was proposed by Lo (2004), in two main Vietnamese stock exchanges by measuring the current stock returns against historical stock returns. To ensure the robustness of the results, the authors run a series of autocorrelation tests—namely, the automatic variance ratio (AVR) test, the automatic portmanteau (AP) test, and the generalized spectral (GS) test—and a time-varying autoregressive approach. They conclude that, because the market efficiency of the Vietnamese stock exchanges varies over time and is influenced by the market conditions, the behavior of the stock market is in line with the adaptive market hypothesis.

With the advent of advanced and automated technologies, companies worldwide face immense pressure to innovate and raise productivity to stay competitive, and, more importantly, afloat. There are undoubtedly many other aspects of entrepreneurial finance in the dawn of Industry 4.0 that are yet to be included in this volume. Nonetheless, through different approaches and outlooks, this collection of articles has altogether contributed to progressing our knowledge of financial risk and management in emerging economies, along with our understanding of all the limitations pertaining to them and the required intellectual honesty (Vuong 2020).

Funding: This research received no external funding.

Acknowledgments: The author thanks the research staff at AISDL (Vuong & Associates, Hanoi, Vietnam) for their support throughout the process.

Conflicts of Interest: The author declares no conflict of interest.

References

Ho, Hai, Hanh Thi Vu, Tien Dao Ngoc, Tung Ho, and Quan-Hoang Vuong. 2019. When the poor buy the rich: New evidence on wealth effects of cross-border acquisitions. *Journal of Risk and Financial Management* 12: 102. [CrossRef]

Koilo, Viktoriia. 2019. Evidence of the Environmental Kuznets Curve: Unleashing the opportunity of Industry 4.0 in emerging economies. *Journal of Risk and Financial Management* 12: 122. [CrossRef]

Lo, Andrew W. 2004. The Adaptive Markets Hypothesis: Market efficiency from an evolutionary perspective. *Journal of Portfolio Management, Forthcoming* 30: 15–29. [CrossRef]

Pham, Thanh-Hang, Manh-Toan Ho, Thu-Trang Vuong, Manh-Cuong Nguyen, and Quan-Hoang Vuong. 2020. Entrepreneurial finance: Insights from English language training market in Vietnam. *Journal of Risk and Financial Management* 13: 96. [CrossRef]

Tran Trung, Dzung Phan, and Hung Pham Quang. 2019. Adaptive Market Hypothesis: Evidence from the Vietnamese stock market. *Journal of Risk and Financial Management* 12: 81. [CrossRef]

Vu, Thi-Hanh, Van-Duy Nguyen, Manh-Tung Ho, and Quan-Hoang Vuong. 2019. Determinants of Vietnamese listed firm performance: Competition, wage, CEO, firm size, age, and international trade. *Journal of Risk and Financial Management* 12: 62. [CrossRef]

Vuong, Quan-Hoang. 2018. The (ir)rational consideration of the cost of science in transition economies. *Nature Human Behaviour* 2: 5. [CrossRef] [PubMed]

Vuong, Quan-Hoang. 2020. Reform retractions to make them more transparent. *Nature* 582: 149. [CrossRef]

Vuong, Quan-Hoang, Manh-Tung Ho, Hong-Kong T. Nguyen, Thu-Trang Vuong, Trung Tran, Khanh-Linh Hoang, Thi-Hanh Vu, Phuong-Hanh Hoang, Minh-Hoang Nguyen, Manh-Toan Ho, and et al. 2020. On how religions could accidentally incite lies and violence: Folktales as a cultural transmitter. *Palgrave Communications* 6: 82. [CrossRef]

© 2020 by the author. Licensee MDPI, Basel, Switzerland. This article is an open access article distributed under the terms and conditions of the Creative Commons Attribution (CC BY) license (http://creativecommons.org/licenses/by/4.0/).

Article

Entrepreneurial Finance: Insights from English Language Training Market in Vietnam

Thanh-Hang Pham [1,2,*], Manh-Toan Ho [3,4], Thu-Trang Vuong [4,5], Manh-Cuong Nguyen [6] and Quan-Hoang Vuong [3,7]

1. Faculty of Management and Tourism, Hanoi University, Km9 Nguyen Trai Road, Thanh Xuan, Hanoi 100803, Vietnam
2. School of Business, RMIT Vietnam University, Hanoi 100000, Vietnam
3. Centre for Interdisciplinary Social Research, Phenikaa University, Yen Nghia Ward, Ha Dong District, Hanoi 100803, Vietnam; toan.homanh@phenikaa-uni.edu.vn (M.-T.H.); hoang.vuongquan@phenikaa-uni.edu.vn (Q.-H.V.)
4. A.I. for Social Data Lab, Vuong & Associates, 3/161 Thinh Quang, Dong Da District, Hanoi 100000, Vietnam; thutrang.vuong@sciencespo.fr
5. École Doctorale, Sciences Po Paris, 75337 Paris, France
6. Faculty of International Studies, Hanoi University, Km9 Nguyen Trai Road, Thanh Xuan, Hanoi 100803, Vietnam; manhcuongvhgd@gmail.com
7. Centre Emile Bernheim, Université Libre de Bruxelles, B-1050 Brussels, Belgium
* Correspondence: hangpt@hanu.edu.vn

Received: 29 March 2020; Accepted: 11 May 2020; Published: 13 May 2020

Abstract: Entrepreneurship plays an indispensable role in the economic development and poverty reduction of emerging economies like Vietnam. The rapid development of technologies during the Fourth Industrial Revolution (Industry 4.0) has a significant impact on business in every field, especially in the innovation-focused area of entrepreneurship. However, the topic of entrepreneurial activities with technology applications in Vietnam is under-researched. In addition, the body of literature regarding entrepreneurial finance tends to focus on advanced economies, while mostly neglecting the contextual differences in developing nations. Therefore, this research contributes to these topics by investigating the main characteristics of a high potential market for entrepreneurs in Vietnam, which is the English language training market (ELTM). It also aims at indicating the impacts of technology on the entrepreneurial firms within this market, with an emphasis on financing sources. To answer the research questions, this study employs a qualitative analysis and conducts 12 in-depth, semi-structured interviews with entrepreneurs and researchers in the field. The key findings in our study highlight the main contributing factors to the growth of the market, both universally and context-specific for a developing nation like Vietnam. It also lists the leaders in each market segment and the industry's potential profit margin. The results also show that most entrepreneurs in the ELTM utilized private sources of finance rather than external ones, such as bank loans. It again confirms the idea from previous works that even with the rapid development of the economic and technological landscape, entrepreneurial activities in general barely benefit from additional sources of funding. However, it also points out the distinct characteristics of the ELTM that may influence these financing issues; for example, English training services usually collect revenues from customers before delivering their classes. This is of advantage for entrepreneurs in this area and helps significantly reduce the financial barriers. These findings, which are among the first attempts to contribute to a better understanding of entrepreneurial opportunities in the Industry 4.0 in Vietnam, provide valuable insights for policymakers and entrepreneurs, as well as investors.

Keywords: entrepreneurship; entrepreneurial finance; Vietnam; English training; entrepreneurial opportunities; edtech; Industry 4.0; finance performance; computational entrepreneurship

1. Introduction

In Vietnam, entrepreneurship has been a major driver of the economy since the overall economic reform known as Doi Moi in 1986 (Vuong 2016, Vuong et al. 2019). The focus on economic renovation and open-door policies have opened up new opportunities for privately owned enterprises. Regardless of forms and sizes, these entrepreneurial ventures have contributed significantly to the development of the economy, as well as giving the people opportunities to have a better living standard (La and Vuong 2019, Andersen and Nielsen 2012). During the mid-1980s, GDP per capita stagnated between US$200 and US$300 (Vanham 2018) but soared to US$6900 in 2017 (Central Intelligence Agency 2020). This leads to the rise of a middle class as a strong catalyst for increased consumer spending (McKinsey & Company 2019), with significant changes in their purchasing behaviors, for example, more substantial investment in education for their children.

Additionally, in the era of globalization, emerging economies, including Vietnam, need to be open and integrated in terms of cross-border trade and investment, thus heightening the need to communicate interculturally using English as the lingua franca (Vuong and Napier 2015). As a result, during the past decades, English has gained its dominance as a foreign language in these nations.

However, for a considerable portion of the Vietnamese population, English proficiency remained limited, with an overall "low" English proficiency ranking compared to other countries (Tuoi Tre News 2019). Therefore, Vietnam's English language training market (ELTM) is considered as promising for entrepreneurial activities (EVBN 2018). The country has a population of nearly 100 million people, including 45.7% of people in the working-age and another 38% from 0–24 years old who have substantial demand for the English language training services (Central Intelligence Agency 2020). This is further supported by a strong commitment by the government to promote English as the primary foreign language (Trines, Stefan, BMI 2019, Bui and Nguyen 2016). Additionally, education has always played a central role in Vietnam's society and culture, as it is seen as the ultimate path to success and as a way to make the family proud (EVBN 2018). The rise of different movements in the education sector, namely outbound education (Trines, Stefan), English as a medium of instruction in universities (BMI 2019) and new transnational or advanced programs in higher education (EVBN 2018), have all contributed to the development of ELTM as a potential landscape for entrepreneurial activities.

Within this landscape of favorable external factors, the ELTM has long developed in the country, with a large number of independent teachers as well as English centers. Recently, with the rapid advancement in technology in the Fourth Industrial Revolution, i.e., Industry 4.0, the education sector in general and the ELTM market, in particular, have witnessed the rapid emergence of new business models to satisfy diverse customer needs. These so-called edtech startups, or education technology, have attracted significant investment, totaling up to US$55 million in 2018, followed by a three-fold rise to US$150 million in 2019 (Tech Collective 2019). Overall, edtech was among the top five most profitable areas for Vietnamese start-ups, with ELTM as one of the most attractive segments. As some typical examples, various firms operating in this market have obtained funding from foreign capital ventures, namely TOPICA Edtech Group with US$50 million (Russell 2018), Yola English teaching school with US$10 million (Nguyen 2019) or ELSA artificial intelligence (AI)-powered startup with US$7 million (Russell 2019). The emergence of these external financial sources may also signal a crucial change in the entrepreneurial finance of the market. As finance is considered as the lifeblood of a business, firms' financial management will also be drastically affected by these upcoming changes in the source of funding (Horák 2016).

Given the rapidly changing landscape of the ELTM in Vietnam, which also represents the same movement in various other developing economies, this research aims at investigating the impacts of technology on the ELTM in Vietnam with a focus on entrepreneurial financing issues and trends in the market. To address the research objective of an exploratory study, this study employs qualitative analysis and conducts 12 in-depth, semi-structured interviews with entrepreneurs and researchers in the field.

2. Literature Review

2.1. Entrepreneurial Finance Research

First, to examine a phenomenon, researchers need to define it and put some boundaries around it. Therefore, in this paper, entrepreneurship is defined as an activity that involves the discovery, evaluation, and exploitation of opportunities to introduce new goods and services, ways of organizing, markets, processes, and raw materials, through organizing efforts that previously had not existed (Venkataraman 1997, Shane and Venkataraman 2000, Shane 2003). This definition is chosen for its popularity in the research field, as well as the inclusiveness that is appropriate for a market consisting of diverse entrepreneurial forms, such as independent teachers, English training centers, or technology-based products and services. Amongst various aspects, such as human capital, social capital, or entrepreneurial behavior that influence entrepreneurial performance (Santarelli and Tran 2013, Tipu and Arain 2011), financial constraints are frequently cited as the main barrier to entrepreneurship (Andersen and Nielsen 2012). By definition, entrepreneurial finance focuses on studying the financial aspects of entrepreneurship, such as financial performance and resource allocation, etc., which deviates from traditional finance studies (Paré et al. 2009). Overall, entrepreneurial finance is a rapidly growing research field, in which different research domains can be found. In the scope of this paper, we would like to focus on the area of alternative sources of capital, as the ability to access capital is among the most critical issues facing entrepreneurial firms.

The state of the art of entrepreneurial finance has recently been examined by several scientists. Denis (2004) stated that as these firms do not yet generate profits and mostly lack tangible assets, they usually cannot rely on debt financing, or in other words, bank loans. Therefore, three primary sources of outside equity financing tend to be utilized, including venture capital funds, angel investors, and corporate investors. The first one refers to "limited partnerships in which the managing partners invest on behalf of the limited partners" (Denis 2004, p. 304). It is stated that an essential difference between venture capital and bank finance is that a VC often provides substantial managerial contributions to the venture (De Bettignies and Brander 2007). The second one refers to "high net worth" people who use their own money to invest in several firms (Denis 2004, p. 304). Lastly, corporate investors conduct investment activities on behalf of their shareholders to aim for strategic and/or financial objectives. It is further stated that, although the accurate division of the total funding into each source is difficult, all these three funding sources make a substantial capital contribution to the entrepreneurial firms (Denis 2004).

In Cumming and Groh (2018) work, they stated several Google Scholar trends for different search terms in entrepreneurial finance, including debt, IPO (initial public offering), venture capital, private equity, angel, entrepreneurial finance, trade credit and crowdfunding (Cumming and Groh 2018). Among these, IPOs and venture capital have been the focus of research in the area from 2000 to 2016, and interest in crowdfunding was basically non-existent until 2020, but since then has grown at a remarkable rate (Cumming and Groh 2018). While IPO is regarded as a critical exit event of venture capital investments, crowdfunding is defined as an entrepreneur's means of collecting capital from an external source represented by a large community (Belleflamme et al. 2014), even before direct sales (Miglo 2020). Cole and Sokolyk (2018) extend previous papers and focus on the two kinds of debt which exist for start-ups: debt originated by the venture (business debt) and debt originated by the entrepreneur (personal debt) (Cole and Sokolyk 2018). The authors find that the distinction between personal debt and business debt is important. Better quality start-ups are more likely to obtain business debt, and such debt is associated with higher survival and revenue growth rates (Cole and Sokolyk 2018).

Bellavitis et al. (2017) discussed these sources in more detail. The study indicated the usual financing cycle, which started with the three "Fs", representing friends, family, and "fools", followed by business angels, VCs, and capital markets (Bellavitis et al. 2017). Entrepreneurs looking to raise seed finance usually turned to their close ties. They developed a prototype, approached the first clients, and hopefully generated revenues. Once these initial milestones were achieved, entrepreneurs started enlarging their circle of financiers with business angels. These wealthy and well-connected individuals usually provided the capital to expand. At this stage, the venture was supposed to grow substantially to be appealing to institutional investors such as VCs, including both domestic and cross-border ones (Bradley et al. 2019). VC funding and connections fuel strong growth domestically and internationally. Once the start-up raised VC funding, the entrepreneur and the investors shared the goal of reaching an IPO or selling the company to a large corporation. The majority of highly successful companies followed a similar funding cycle (Berger and Udell 1998). Nowadays, however, this funding cycle has to be re-conceptualized. Entrepreneurs in science and technology start-ups can raise finance from new sources, including accelerators and incubators, proof-of-concept centers, university-based seed funds, and crowdfunding platforms. Undeniably, VC, and angels are important sources of financing for entrepreneurial ventures. However, only an extremely select group of entrepreneurial firms with high-growth ambitions are able to attract VC or angel financing. Moreover, interestingly, studies have suggested—contrary to the commonly held view in entrepreneurial finance literature—that banks and debt finance represent a major source of financing for entrepreneurial firms (Cassar 2004, Zarutskie 2006, Huyghebaert and Van de Gucht 2007).

Overall, these works, together with various others, call for more research into entrepreneurial finance to shed light on newly emerging phenomena, given the practical importance of entrepreneurial finance for developed, as well as developing economies. Furthermore, with the dominance of studies examining entrepreneurship in advanced countries (Vuong et al. 2020, Meyer et al. 2014), additional insights into the phenomena within emerging economies' context may also be of critical value to advance the discipline.

2.2. Entrepreneurship Research Regarding Vietnam Context

The study by Vuong et al. (2020) highlighted the strong wave of entrepreneurial activities in Vietnam (Vuong et al. 2020). It was also stated that cultural influence might be the reason why much of the non-innovative working culture in enterprises across the country has persisted so long. It is common for entrepreneurs to start businesses by initially copying the model from other existing firms and amending them later to adjust to the changing environment. Findings have also revealed that the majority of business founders in Vietnam base their initial settings on personal intuition and pure luck, without any analytical plan being carried out (Vuong et al. 2020). Strikingly, the study indicates that although Industry 4.0 and Artificial Intelligence have become the buzzwords in both governmental agendas and public discussions in recent years (Viet Nam News 2018), the technological application is nearly absent from much of the research on entrepreneurship in Vietnam. From 2008 to 2018, there have only been three research articles that can be classified into the topic of technological utilization, namely Thao and Swierczek (2008), Le et al. (2018); Le et al. (2012). The first one investigates the way small and medium-sized travel agencies, in the role of business customers, perceive the benefits as well as limitations of Internet use relating to relationship development and loyalty with their service suppliers (Thao and Swierczek 2008). The second one examines technological gaps and the factors affecting variations in the technical efficiency of small and medium enterprises (SMEs) in Vietnam (Le et al. 2018). The last one employs an adaptation of the technology—organization—environment framework and test a model of e-commerce adoption in a number of internal and external factors identified in empirical studies (Le et al. 2012). However, none of those studies mention high-tech applications such as machine learning, artificial intelligence, etc.

In another recent systematic review of 111 entrepreneurship studies regarding Vietnam's context, the results show that from 2013, the promotion of entrepreneurship in Vietnamese society has pushed the interest of Vietnamese people, and consequently, researchers and research productivity (Vuong et al. 2020). Before 2012, academics were not enthusiastic about entrepreneurship; the increase of public attention on the subject has driven their focus to the field. The study also pointed at the difference between Vietnamese entrepreneurship research compared to the global landscape. While the former tends to examine practical aspects of entrepreneurial activities, the latter focuses more on the cognitive and theoretical aspects of entrepreneurship. In particular, 40 articles, accounting for more than one-third of this body of literature, are concerned with managing firms' capital and economic efficiency. These studies highlight the heavy reliance of Vietnamese SMEs on financial capital, so much that capital constraint was seen as the biggest concern for enterprises. Besides, the study by Vuong et al. (2020) again highlights the lack of research on some important topics, especially in terms of technology application (Vuong et al. 2020).

These studies conclude that the status of entrepreneurship research in Vietnam is still in its infancy, both in terms of output as well as the content. On the one hand, the findings show a substantial interest in the aspect of entrepreneurial finance in Vietnam's context; on the other hand, it also calls for more studies on under-researched topics on entrepreneurship, including practical matters such as technology application.

2.3. Overview of Vietnam's English Language Training Market

Vietnam's ELTM is considered as a potential area for entrepreneurial opportunities. According to BMI Global, in 2019, 437 projects with a total registered foreign investment of USD 4.3 billion were reported in the education and training sector, the majority of which has been directed towards the English language training area (BMI 2019). In the two biggest cities of Vietnam, namely Hanoi and Ho Chi Minh cities, the number of registered language centers have increased significantly. In 2018, Hanoi had approximately 500 English language centers, and this number soared by 80% to around 900 in the following year (Department of Education and Training Hanoi 2018, 2019). In Ho Chi Minh city, there was a growth of 50% from 400 English centers in 2017 to 600 in 2019 (Department of Education and Training 2017, 2019). This shows the timely initiatives of entrepreneurs to grasp opportunities in this market.

Various factors have contributed to the significant development of the ELTM in Vietnam. The economic outlook in the medium term is positive, with the GDP growth rate in the last two years exceeding 7% (The World Bank Vietnam 2020). Furthermore, Vietnam continues to actively integrate into the global economy by joining WTO in 2007 and various free trade agreements with other countries (Central Intelligence Agency 2020) The country has attracted a steady inflow of foreign direct investment (FDI), reaching US$15.5 billion in 2018 (The World Bank 2020). These factors contribute to the rapid growth of demand in language training, as both domestic and international companies prefer candidates with higher proficiency in the foreign language. Together with that, an emerging middle class, currently accounting for 13% of the population, is expected to amount to 44 million people in 2020 and reach 26% of the population by 2026 (The World Bank Vietnam 2020, ANT Consulting 2020). This middle-income group creates strong purchasing power in the market, such as for studying and traveling abroad (EVBN 2018).

Having a population of nearly 99 million people, Vietnam is considered as a nation of the "golden age," with 45.7% people in the working-age. Also, the number of students from kindergarten to higher education adds up to almost 23 million, many of whom have English as a compulsory subject at school, as the medium of instruction or as a critical asset for recruitment opportunities. With policies urging for the enhancement of English proficiency for Vietnamese people, this creates an enormous market for entrepreneurs. In terms of technological use, this young population has excessive usage of the Internet. In 2018, there were 64 million Internet users and a digital economy value of US$ 9 billion. The e-commerce value accounts for 1.7% of GDP, with a value of US$3.5 billion (Anh 2020).

Moreover, Vietnam's society and culture, which is rooted in Confucianism, has always valued education as the key to success (Vuong et al. 2018, 2020, 2020). Teachers are highly regarded in Vietnam and parents are willing to go to great lengths to ensure that their children receive a good education, as commented by Minister of Education Phung Xuan Nha: "Vietnamese parents can sacrifice everything, sell their houses and land just to give their children an education" (McKinsey & Company 2019). In terms of the education service, it is stated that the private education section is preferred over public schools because it is perceived as providing better teaching methods as well as improved results for learners (EVBN 2018). This perspective results in a robust demand for 'non-public', 'supplementary', and 'overseas' services.

Regarding government policies, in the early 2000s, English was claimed to become a compulsory subject for all students throughout the country (Prime Minister 2001). Since then, the government has been opening doors for a broad spectrum of international universities, corporations, and non-government organizations (NGOs) to collaboratively promote English in Vietnam. Higher investment incentives also apply for foreign investment in this sector than other foreign investment forms (British Business Group Vietnam 2018). In particular, the Vietnamese government specifies that education is one of the prioritized areas; as a result, investment in the field can enjoy a 10% tax reduction for the entire lifetime of operation, application for all projects. Enterprises in this sector also benefit from four years of corporate income tax (CIT) exemption and five years of 50% reduction on payable CIT (BMI 2019).

In terms of potential customers, the major customer segments of English language training services all show positive signals. For K-12 students, Vietnam's curriculum for junior and senior secondary schools requires English to be taught as a compulsory subject from grade 6 to grade 12. A pilot program was implemented in 2010 and 2011 to teach the language as a compulsory subject from Grade 3. Overall, the importance of English can be seen through its vital role in final and entrance exams at middle school and tertiary levels (Bui and Nguyen 2016). Another contributing factor is the emergence of international schools in Vietnam, with a total of 123 English-medium schools, accommodating more than 66,000 students and earning tuition fee income of around US$634 million (BMI 2019). For higher education, Vietnam is regarded as one of the most dynamic markets for studying abroad in the world, with an explosion of the number of outbound students by 680 percent during the period from 1999 to 2016 (Trines, Stefan). It was reported that there were more than 946,000 students in 2017 (UNESCO Institute of Statistics 2020). It is further predicted that student mobility is guaranteed to grow in the coming years, particularly in the context of Vietnam's internationalization in both the economy and the education system (Trines, Stefan). Domestically, new university programs besides the standard one, namely high-quality, advanced, and transnational programs (EVBN 2018), have been introduced, most of which use English as a medium of instruction and provide opportunities to transfer to partner universities abroad. Therefore, applicants are required to have a certain English level, and these programs also make the language a requirement for students to graduate. These outbound, as well as domestic, trends in education all enhance the importance of English and motivate learners to find ways to improve their level of the language.

As for the workforce, English has always been regarded as an essential skill in employment and promotion opportunities. Additional attributes, including language proficiency and soft skills, are highly appreciated in the country, because of their ability to increase individuals' employability (EVBN 2018). The report *Vietnam 2035: toward prosperity, creativity, equity, and democracy*, jointly prepared by the Ministry of Planning and Investment and the World Bank Group, asserts that the country must develop its human capital in terms of technical skills and especially strong English language skills. By getting a better level of English proficiency, particularly in specialized topics, it will help to narrow the skill gaps of Vietnam's labor force compared to the international standards, which will result in better opportunities for the nation (World Bank Group 2016).

These favorable conditions for ELTM contrast with the situation of Vietnamese people's limited English level. The country's English skills were listed in the low-proficiency category in 2019 in The English Proficiency Index, with data from more than 2,300,000 test-takers (Tuoi Tre News 2019, Education First 2019). Additionally, the average English score of high school graduates in the national exam in 2019 was only 4.36/10, with a below-average score in two-thirds of the students (Phan 2019). As for the workforce, Vietnam was ranked 57th out of 76 countries surveyed in the Total Workforce Index Report in 2019, a significant fall from the previous year ranking of 43rd. One of the three challenges faced by the nation's labor force is stated to be low English proficiency. The limited language level remains one barrier that prevents the country from moving upstream in the global value chain

(Nguyen 2020). These data show a low level of English proficiency among Vietnamese people, which signals a need to improve their skills by soliciting formal and non-formal education services.

Based on the discussed factor, Vietnam's ELTM is considered as highly promising for entrepreneurial opportunities. Therefore, more efforts should be made to investigate this market and its characteristics, as well as the particular entrepreneurial finance aspect of start-ups.

2.4. Research Questions

Given the context of Vietnam's ELTM, as well as the lack of studies about Vietnam's entrepreneurship, especially with a focus on financial and technology application aspects, this research aims to answer the following research questions:

1. What are the main characteristics of ELTM in Vietnam?
2. What are the impacts of technology on entrepreneurial firms, especially entrepreneurial finance, in ELTM in Vietnam?

3. Method and Material

3.1. Method

To answer the research questions, given the infancy of the entrepreneurship literature about Vietnam's context, especially with no previous work focusing on technology application in ELTM, this study adopts an exploratory qualitative design. In particular, semi-structured in-depth interviews were used to collect information from two groups, namely education researchers and entrepreneurs in the ELTM. This research design is chosen because semi-structured schedules enable the examination of spontaneous expressions, reducing pre-conceptualized boundaries, and simultaneously keeping to the interview agenda (Cavaco et al. 2005). In addition, the flexibility of a semi-structured interview with exploratory questions helps a researcher to understand the world from the participant's perspective (Cavaco et al. 2005; Charlton and Barrow 2002; Robson 2002; Kvale 1996).

Firstly, the research team had to identify a small group of target participants on a convenience basis. These respondents were supposed to have diverse perspectives on the research topic. Then, they were asked to recommend other participants for interviews. The selection criteria were that the education researchers have insights into the subject matter, and the entrepreneurs have been directly involved in the ELTM. This is known as the snowball sampling technique (Quinn Patton 2002), which is cost-effective and quite efficient in getting a suitable sample group for a qualitative investigation. However, the main drawback of this sampling method is its non-probability and non-randomness. As a result, conclusions produced relate only to the participants' perceptions and situations, but that does not mean that the insights revealed are irrelevant to an understanding of the experiences of a larger group. It is crucial, though, that any transfer of ideas from this research to other settings is done by the reader, and not by the investigator (Lincoln and Guba 1985). The interviews took place during February and March 2020. The research team continued the data collection until the saturation point of data, where no novel insights emerged from the interviewees. Nearly 20 interviews were conducted, of which some had to be canceled, as the participants did not meet the selection criteria. Finally, 12 interviews were chosen for the data analysis of this research.

A thematic analysis was used to organize the interview material in relation to the research questions (Banister 2011). The main themes were examined and discussed informally, which gave insight into how to approach the analysis. The discourse was then categorized into a concise and structured format, which gave a clear overview of the main themes (Robson 2002); this, in turn, allowed the comparison of differences and similarities between respondents. Throughout the analysis, reference was made to the original transcripts.

3.2. Material

The detailed profile of 12 participants is presented in Table A1, in which each person receives a number to protect their anonymity. The form of interviews was implemented in the most preferred way by the participants. Most of them were conducted face-to-face in person. Several others were conducted by telephone, and in one case, the questions were sent via email to the participant, and answers were sent back. Regardless of the form, the interviews were successful in getting a "rich, detailed, and concrete description" (Quinn Patton 2002). This is crucial to a successful qualitative investigation.

Based on instructions from Spradley (2016), most of the questions in the interviews were open-ended, with no limits on how each participant would share their perspectives (Quinn Patton 2002). Following the participants' responses, more questions can be asked to clarify or further investigate these responses.

To answer the first research question about the main characteristics of ELTM in Vietnam, the following questions were asked:

- What factors have been affecting the development of ELTM in Vietnam?
- What companies are the market leaders in ELTM in Vietnam?
- What is the average profit margin of enterprises participating in the ELTM in Vietnam?
- How do you evaluate the ELTM in Vietnam in the next five years?

To answer the second research question about the impacts of technology on entrepreneurial firms, especially entrepreneurial finance in ELTM in Vietnam, the following questions were asked:

- How does technology affect the ELTM in Vietnam?
- How does technology affect entrepreneurial opportunities in the ELTM in Vietnam?
- How do enterprises in the ELTM in Vietnam finance their businesses?
- Does technology change the way enterprises in the ELTM in Vietnam finance their businesses?

Some questions were only asked for participants who were the business owners of firms operating in the ELTM, including:

- How does technology affect your firm's business operations?
- How did you finance your business?
- Does technology affect the way you finance your business?

The language used in all interviews was Vietnamese, as this is the native language for both the participants and the authors. For telephone and in-person interviews, with permission from the interviewees, the authors kept a digital record for each of them for further reference. During the meetings, all necessary care was taken to make sure that the respondents were not exposed to any risks, in terms of both emotional and reputational aspects.

4. Findings

In this part, key themes from the interviews are presented. Participants are referred to as researchers or entrepreneurs. To preserve the authenticity of participants' comments, translation into English of the actual words or phrases used by participants are reported.

4.1. Main Characteristics of ELTM in Vietnam

The themes related to the main characteristics of the ELTM in Vietnam can be divided into two parts, namely the factors affecting the growth of ELTM and market leaders, as well as the profit margin of the ELTM.

4.1.1. Factors Affecting the Growth of ELTM

The participants were invited to comment on the driving forces of the ELTM in recent years. It was the case that one participant after another reported customer demand as one of the most critical factors affecting the rapid development of the ELTM. It was further explained by Participant 2 that for children, the demand mainly comes from parents, especially mothers, who have the tendency to discuss their children's schooling and education. This phenomenon is further promoted via discussions on online platforms, previously as online forums, and more recently as social media groups, where ideas can be shared easily. This results in the fact that customer demands are more easily expressed, whereas recommendations or reviews of education services can be more rapidly shared among group members. For teenagers, students, and adults, the influence of social media was also highlighted, for example, in participant 11's comment:

> Facebook pages affect the development of ELTM as they share inspirational posts every day, so even if one person does not have the motivation in the first place when they continuously see people and friends around them learn English, they also have the tendency to be eager to learn.

Another factor that was reported by many participants is the impact of globalization and the strong economic integration of Vietnam into the global market. Because of this significant trend, English, as a lingua franca, has become an essential tool for any worker in the economy. Participant 6's view reflected the ideas reported by many of other participants:

> Firms target the working people that want to improve their English skills. The ultimate goal is to get better job opportunities.

Furthermore, government policies were referred to by more than half of the participants. In accordance with the setting mentioned above, the National Foreign Language Project 2020 was considered one particularly crucial program to enhance the role of English as a foreign language in the education system.

The prevailing view of participants was that technology is another significant contributing factor to the growth of the market. It affects various aspects of the market, such as promoting the products and services more effectively, as well as organizing the learning experience more quickly.

Comments made by some participants also revealed that the availability of learning and teaching material was another factor influencing the growth of ELTM. With the abundance of materials both online and in printed editions, teachers and language training centers have a variety of choices about which one suits their teaching purpose and learning path for students. The significant reduction in price, especially with online sources, also results in families being more willing to buy books and materials for their children.

Interestingly, one participant saw the development of online teaching partly as a result of terrible traffic in big cities in Vietnam, as reported:

> The reason why online English training can invade the market and grow is because of terrible traffic, especially in big cities. Learners cannot stand going such a long way through many traffic congestion points. They are afraid of traffic accidents, kidnapping, and other dangers on the street. Children nowadays are precious to their parents, so safety is the most important thing.

Overall, the participants' accounts regarding factors that affect the development of ELTM focused on four main aspects: customer demand, globalization, government policies, and technology. For each customer segment, primarily based on age groups, other additional factors help contribute to the growth of the market over recent decades.

4.1.2. Market Leaders and Profit Margin

It was widely commented that there was no reliable source of information and statistics about the industry, so it was not transparent enough to state which company is the market leader. However, in each market segment, some brands were mentioned by various participants. In the online ELTM,

TOPICA Native was reported by all participants as the leading firm in the sector of general English for working people. Participant 4 regarded TOPICA as the "game-changer" of the market, as it changes customers' habits remarkably. Besides, Monkey Junior was considered the most popular application of learning English for kids. On the other hand, in terms of offline market penetration, APAX, with 123 branches, was claimed to be the biggest chain of English training centers. Various participants also reported on another criterion of evaluation, which is the long history of the brand, in which some names appear to be repeated in the accounts, including British Council, Apollo, Language Link, and ILA.

The participants were also invited to comment on the average profit margin of firms operating in the ELTM in Vietnam. Interestingly, the accounts here were quite diverse. For traditional business models, the dominating comment was that profit margin ranges from 25% to 30%. However, some participants even reported a range from 20% to 50%, and when asked further to explain the reason for such a big gap, participant 5 responded by saying:

> Many English language training centers have brilliant strategies to cut costs. The main reason is that they have a low-cost human resource. For a center, hiring foreign teachers is the biggest cost item, with an hourly rate from US$22 to US$30. If the centers hire 100% foreign teachers, and also provide the service of outsourcing these teachers, only this service helps them break even and bring about additional profits besides the profits from their own classes. However, if firms spend resources on recruiting foreign teachers even though this is not their strength, the profit margin will be quite low.

For high-tech firms in the ELTM in Vietnam, comments from the participants were even more polarized. On the one hand, a small group of participants reported positively about this segment, for example, participant 2 also stated that "for firms focusing on online markets, the profit margin is around 40%–45%." On the other hand, participants who are running firms in this market segment shared different ideas; in particular, participant 3 reported that "online teaching models currently cannot generate profits." Participant 6 expressed a similar point of view, adding that:

> Start-up businesses do not focus on profit margin. Instead, their focus is on market growth and scale. Therefore, revenues generated will be used for reinvesting, which is different from the traditional business model. However, the revenue growth rate will be high, around 20% monthly.

Overall, it can be seen from participants' comments that there is no dominating market leader in the whole ELTM in Vietnam, and each company mentioned appears to have competitive advantages in certain aspects. Together with that, the profit margin of offline business models is quite favorable if firms can manage to survive after the early stage of establishment. On the other hand, online-focused companies now prioritize growth and market share rather than gaining profits.

4.2. Impacts of Technology on Entrepreneurial Firms and Entrepreneurial Finance in ELTM in Vietnam

The themes related to the impacts of technology on entrepreneurial firms and entrepreneurial finance in ELTM in Vietnam can be divided into several parts. First, the impacts on entrepreneurial opportunities are discussed; then, the effects on operations and financing of firms in the ELTM are discussed.

4.2.1. Technology and Entrepreneurial Opportunities in English Language Training Market

When asked about entrepreneurial opportunities in ELTM in Vietnam, most of the participants evaluated the opportunities as "promising" and "high potential." Participant 2 even commented that "the entry barrier to this market is nearly zero." On the other hand, two participants reported the same positive viewpoint about setting up a business in the market, yet added that surviving in this fiercely competitive market is a different thing.

Participant 1 shared a slightly different idea that the opportunities now are more complicated than previously, and only firms that can take advantage of technology and adopt effective business models will be able to grasp these opportunities.

In terms of market segments that are the most promising, participants' points of view were quite diverse. Participant 6 reported that:

> In all segments of the market, there is no dominating firms or brands. Opportunities exist because the demand for learning is high.

Participant 3 expressed a different point of view that traditional, offline-focused business models are much more comfortable than the online segment because, in the latter, even big corporations are still struggling, for example, TOPICA Native.

From another perspective, participant 9 saw the matter as highly promising opportunities for niche demand, for instance, customizing products and services and offering individualized care for each learner. Large enterprises that focus on economies of scale may find it challenging to meet this type of demand, therefore leaving these niche segments open for entrepreneurs.

The participants' accounts regarding the application of technologies strongly suggested that these new advancements are significantly useful for entrepreneurs. For example, some participants provided details about the ease and convenience of running a business with a single device, which was impossible just a few years ago. Small business owners or independent teachers can reach customers/students, market their services, provide consultations, and deliver lessons on their smartphones, with the support of different technological tools. Moreover, it was not uncommon for the participant to refer to technology integration as a way to cut costs, such as the costs of printing and teaching material. Students can use online sources to support their learning or even replace traditional textbooks and worksheets. The existence of a gap between different customer segments was, however, acknowledged. One participant was especially detailed in his remarks.

> In big cities, technology applications can be useful. However, in rural areas, people's perceptions are very different; they never let their children use technologies in that way, nor do they have the equipment and facilities to do so.

Participant 6, though running a company developing applications to help kids learn English, reported explicitly that

> Starting up a business does not necessarily rely on technologies. I have friends who use traditional business models and still win their niche market. However, technologies can help firms to scale up rapidly.

Not immediately evident in these remarks, but consistent with the tone in which they were communicated, was the message that combines both offline and online features was a promising option for starting up in the ELTM market.

Though the matter was not explored systematically with the participants, it did generally appear that many participants thought about technology applications and solutions, not as direct competitors of traditional language centers. Participant 6 saw the matter as:

> Technology helps explore new customer segments, increase customer demand, and expand the market as a whole. English learners always face the problem of pricing and affordability. The costs to learn at English centers are too high. Some people who can afford that service cannot find nearby centers to send their kids, either. Technology enables learners to study anywhere, anytime, at affordable prices.

In short, participants generally assessed entrepreneurial opportunities in ELTM in Vietnam positively. Technology plays the role of primarily creating a platform for those opportunities, or partly facilitate the more accessible and cheaper establishment of firms in the market.

4.2.2. Technology and Operations of Firms in English Language Training Market

Another critical theme emerged from the in-depth interviews with participants: the impacts of technology on operations of firms in ELTM in Vietnam. Participant 1's remarks captured most of the elements referred to by others:

> Technological applications primarily affect two critical aspects of business: management and delivering products/services to customers.

In particular, all of the participants who are business owners reported that they are applying technology in their business operations to some extent, from the primary level, such as communicating with students via email and correcting student homework via Google docs, to using business management systems to coordinate activities among departments. Participant 4 reported that:

> Soft-wares for customer relationship management (CRM) or enterprise resource planning (ERP) helps manage learners and internal control of firms more effectively. These systems coordinate all departments of the company so that the owners can monitor the operations of those departments and detect where the problems come from.

Participant 2 want one step further, claiming that:

> Cramming models with one teacher and hundreds of students gradually deteriorated, not so popular as in former times. Franchising one center into a chain of centers becomes more manageable with the help of technology, not only in terms of learning and teaching, but it is about technologies in operations – center organization, customer service, and sales.

In addition, participant 9 highlighted the use of social networks as a highly useful marketing tool for firms and entrepreneurs in the market. She stated that

> Even young teachers can start their own business and using these online channels to promote their personal brands.

Several other participants made similar comments.

In terms of delivering the products or services, various participants regarded technology as a means to improve the quality of English language training services. For online teaching, in former times, teachers and students used applications like Skype, which assisted the real-time conversation and videos of both sides. Technology advancement nowadays enables more functions to facilitate the interaction between teachers and learners, such as the participation of all students in the class, sharing the screen of any members, or direct writing and drawing on the screen. Participant 3 commented on this improvement as:

> This makes the learning experience more "real." Learners will feel like this is not so much different from offline learning, and they will gradually build trust in this form of delivery.

Additionally, of interest here is that all the participants mentioned the COVID-19 pandemic as a critical factor in promoting online learning and creating changes in the way businesses develop their products. For more details, the outbreak has resulted in school and educational service closure in most parts of the country since early February 2020 (La et al. 2020). Some participants reported the challenges, such as participant 5:

> This outbreak [negatively] affects all centers, especially those without any online teaching platform like us.

In short, participants reported the useful application of technology in firms' operations, as well as the way in which they deliver their services and products to customers. The outbreak of COVID-19 globally in 2020 also contributed significantly to the wider spread of this application.

4.2.3. Technology and Financing of Firms in English Language Training Market

Interestingly, a consensus was reached amongst participants about the source of financing among firms in ELTM. In particular, the majority of participants commented that the source of funding for entrepreneurial firms depends on the size of the firm as well as the nature of business. All the participants claimed that small firms obtained their initial capital from the personal saving of the founder or founding team, as well as loans from their family and friends. On the other hand, big-sized enterprises or chains of centers usually raise capital from investment funds. For technology-based companies, it is claimed by some participants that the funding also comes from raising money from angel investors and then investment funds, however, "successful cases in raising this kind of capital in Vietnam are rare." (Participant 6)

Participant 4 commented:

The source of financing is another advantage of running businesses in education, as it does not require substantial capital. The starting point can be minimal, but in a successive way, [which means that] we can collect money before the start of each class, for example. Also, this is an intangible product, the better we do branding for it, the more value it gets.

Another participant further commented:

As a source of financing, bank loans are minimal and insignificant. The reason is that the requirements and procedures [to get a bank loan] are so complicated.

More strikingly, for the majority of the participants, their original source of funding was actually from their savings and support from their families and close friends. Even the founder of an edtech company reported receiving no financial support from any other sources, other than those during their development. Some participants went even one step further, claiming that they started from zero capital. The reason they gave for this irregular opinion is that in the education business, revenues are usually collected before delivering the service. Therefore, this amount of money can be used immediately to cover the costs. The hourly rent of a classroom is also readily available in Vietnamese markets, enabling entrepreneurs to set up their services with little cost. By utilizing this advantage, many young independent teachers have been able to start their own business from literally nothing.

Regarding the impacts of technology on funding source of enterprises in the English training market in Vietnam, participant 2 reported that:

There is no change in the funding sources; it only helps businesses to acquire users and growing market share. Access to financing sources will become more accessible with a larger market share.

Many other participants shared similar viewpoints. Only two participants emphasized that technology would directly impact the online part of the market, in particular edtech companies, which need substantial sources of capital. Participant 6 also mentioned another aspect that venture capital companies would engage in the market, as they prefer business models that are scalable and have the potential to grow exponentially.

Overall, comments of participants about financing sources of firms in ELTM in Vietnam revealed that in the first place, startups mainly based on their savings or loans from family and friends to finance their newly established firms. Technology-based models may seek investments from venture capital later when they reach a certain level of market share and growth. Therefore, generally speaking, technology does not change the funding sources for ELTM, except for the edtech firms.

5. Discussion and Implications

5.1. Discussion

Among the various factors that influence economic growth, it is widely accepted that entrepreneurship plays a crucial role in fostering growth and improved standards of living (Ahlstrom et al. 2019, Ahlstrom 2010, Urbano et al. 2019). As a typical example, Vietnam's "economic miracle", as commented by the World Economic Forum (World Economic Forum 2020), has been relying substantially on SMEs, whose growth in number and capital over the past two decades has cemented entrepreneurship as the backbone of the economy (Vuong et al. 2020). However, research on entrepreneurship in this fast-growing economy is limited in terms of both research output and content (Vuong et al. 2020). Especially when it comes to the topic of technology integration, few works that examine the impacts of this inevitable trend on entrepreneurial firms can be found (Vuong et al. 2020, 2020). On the other hand, the body of literature regarding entrepreneurial finance also lacks diversity in terms of an institutional, socio-economic and cultural context, with the current focus on advanced industrialized English- speaking countries such as the United States, the United Kingdom and Canada (Vuong et al. 2020). Therefore, this research contributes to the body of Vietnamese entrepreneurship literature as well as entrepreneurial finance by investigating the ELTM in Vietnam under the impacts of technology utilization, with a focus on financing issues and trends in the market. The ELTM market was chosen for its high potential; as long as the demand for language training persists and the country's language performance remains average, there is market space for entrants who possess expertise in the field (EVBN 2018).

Generally, the macro-environmental factors of Vietnam positively affect the development of the market, especially regarding government policies to promote English and Vietnamese cultural tradition, which values education as the key to success. More particularly, the primary customer segments of the market have witnessed supportive trends. For K-12 students, the national curriculum for all levels of schools gradually integrated English in terms of both earlier starting grade, as well as more emphasis on its importance. The emergence of international schools in various cities and provinces in the country also means that more and more students will study subjects in English. For higher education students, the strong trends of studying abroad, English as a medium of instruction, and new university programs all contributed to more student demand for English teaching products and services. Last but not least, better employment and promotion opportunities have motivated the workforce to improve themselves. Therefore, the ever-increasing demand from these customer segments for English skills in the country presents enormous possibilities for start-ups and investment in English training centers that meet these needs (Vietnam Economic Times 2020).

To investigate, the research questions were as follows:

1. What are the main characteristics of ELTM in Vietnam?
2. What are the impacts of technology on entrepreneurial firms, especially entrepreneurial finance, in ELTM in Vietnam?

The study's exploratory qualitative design aims at documenting the opinions and perspectives of a selected sample of researchers and entrepreneurs to shed light on these issues. The selection criteria were that the education researchers have insights into the subject matter, and the entrepreneurs have been directly involved in the ELTM. These participants, therefore, cannot represent all stakeholders' perspectives at large. However, they would be able to provide insights related to several matters of specific interest to the investigation, including factors affecting the growth of ELTM, its market leaders and profit margin, technology, and entrepreneurial opportunities, operations of firms, and their financing in ELTM in Vietnam. The data for investigation were obtained by individual, in-depth, semi-structured interviews with the selected participants.

Various themes that emerged from participants' accounts have been highlighted in the paper.

To answer the first research question, participants' comments about the main characteristics of Vietnam's ELTM were collected. Participants, when asked about the main driving forces for the ELTM, listed major factors, such as customer demand, globalization, government policies, and technology. These are consistent with the literature regarding the overview of the ELTM in Vietnam (EVBN 2018, Trines, Stefan, BMI 2019, Bui and Nguyen 2016, British Business Group Vietnam 2018). Interestingly, some specific points directly related to the context of a developing country were also made; for example, traffic congestion and accidents were reported, by participants, to be contributing to the choice of online learning mode for a group of customers. This shows that socio-economic and cultural factors do have an influence on entrepreneurial activities by creating new customer demand. Additionally, similar to the market overview, ELTM is evaluated by most participants as a promising industry that offers potential opportunities for entrepreneurs (EVBN 2018, Trines, Stefan, British Business Group Vietnam 2018). With the favorable profit margin from at least 20% and little sensitivity to the fluctuation of the macro-economic environment, the market appears to be a good investment option during both good and bad times. The integration and application of technology have created even more potential for individuals who can take advantage of these advancements to create a platform for their businesses or to facilitate business operations as well as the delivery of products and services to customers. However, the use of more updated Industry 4.0 technologies, such as virtual reality or artificial intelligence, is still limited.

To have a better understanding of the market landscape, the question about the market leaders was raised. This type of information currently lacks from the body of literature about ELTM in Vietnam. Though no official statistics and market reports are available to the public, participants shared somehow similar accounts about the market leaders. The brand names mentioned were TOPICA Native for the online English teaching for adults, Monkey Junior for online English application for kids, APAX Leaders as the biggest chain of centers, and British Council Vietnam, Apollo English, Language Link Vietnam and ILA as having a long history and reputation for quality. These provide valuable models for entrepreneurs to investigate and analyze before entering the market. The closer look at financing sources as well as financial management of these firms may also be of interest to entrepreneurs or investors to understand the typical business models of leading Vietnamese companies in ELTM.

More details about these companies can be found in Table 1.

To answer the second research question, participants' accounts regarding the impacts of technology on entrepreneurial firms, especially entrepreneurial finance in ELTM in Vietnam, were reported. Generally, technological applications affect two critical areas of ELTM: the way business operations are managed, and the way firms deliver their services and products to customers. More or less, all business owners participating in the study reported the use of technologies in both aspects. However, besides various favorable factors, the application of Industry 4.0 in ELTM in Vietnam has several obstacles. The infrastructure of the country is still limited, which causes interruption during the interaction between teachers and students. This may result in students' loss of eagerness and deterioration of the learning atmosphere within the class. Additionally, if online learning is conducted for kids, it requires parents to spend time and effort to support their kids along the way. Many Vietnamese parents are not familiar with and willing to do this. In terms of geographical areas, the development of online English learning appears to be healthy only in big cities, where Internet facilities, as well as consumer readiness, are much better than less-developed areas.

In terms of entrepreneurial finance in Vietnam's ELTM, the consensus among participants about the entrepreneurial financing source in ELTM was a striking feature of the study, revealing that the majority of small-sized entrepreneurial firms in this market relied on personal savings or loans from family and friends. This is similar to the argument by Bellavitis et al. (2017) that the financing cycle usually started with the three "Fs" representing friends, family, and "fools" (Bellavitis et al. 2017). The personal loans from family and friends can be referred to as personal debt (Cole and Sokolyk 2018). This shows that the start-ups in ELTM seem to be of insufficient quality, as better quality entrepreneurial firms have a better chance to get business debt, and such debt is associated with higher survival and revenue growth rates (Cole and Sokolyk 2018). On the other hand, this study's findings are inconsistent with the results of several previous studies, mainly conducted in developed economies. The three primary sources of outside equity financing by Denis (2004), namely venture capital funds, angel investors, or corporate investors, were not the preferred funding form by Vietnamese entrepreneurs in this market (Denis 2004). This may stem from the infancy stage of the ELTM in Vietnam, in which most entrepreneurial firms are in its early stages. In fact, the only firm in this market that has been listed on the stock exchange is Apax Holdings Investment Joint Stock Company (stock code IBC on Ho Chi Minh Stock Exchange), which is also the owner of the largest English language training center chain in Vietnam, APAX Leaders (Nhung 2020). Similar to this market situation, participants' comments regarding entrepreneurial finance in Vietnam's ELTM mentioned the only exceptions of not using personal savings and loans as the chain of centers and edtech firms. These ventures might seek substantial sources of funding from the beginning to provide resources for them to adopt the strategy of market penetration and to rapidly gain market share. Therefore, they may seek funding from angel investors or venture capital, not only to gain access to financial resources but also to take advantage of their connections and managerial contributions (De Bettignies and Brander 2007, Bellavitis et al. 2017). However, it should be noted that chains of English centers typically start from one single center only. Hence, it is likely that, only after reaching a certain level of development, they would be interested in attracting more finance from external sources.

Table 1. Leading companies in ELTM in Vietnam.

No.	Company	Website	Year of Establishment	Number of Branches	Main Product Lines	Main Target Customer Segment
1	TOPICA Native	https://topicanative.edu.vn/	2014	N/A	Communicative English for beginners Intensive communicative English Communicative English (for corporates)	Working people with communication purposes
2	Monkey Junior	https://www.monkeyjunior.vn/	2014	N/A	Monkey Junior Money Stories Monkey Math VMonkey	Kids 0–10 years old
3	APAX Leaders	https://www.apaxleaders.edu.vn/	2015	123	Apax explorer Apax challenger Apax Conqueror Apax 4.0	4–18-year-old students
4	British Council Vietnam	https://www.britishcouncil.vn/en	2002 (open first ELT courses in Hanoi and Ho Chi Minh City)	5	English for primary English for secondary (grades 6 – 9) English for upper secondary and IELTS English for IELTS preparation English for adults	Kids from 6 years old Adults
5	Apollo English	https://apollo.e	1995	39	Apollo English Junior Apollo English 360 Teacher Training	Kids from 3 years old Adults Teachers
6	Language Link Academic	https://llv.edu.vn/	1996	10	English for very young learners English for young learners English for teens English for university test preparation English for IELTS English for professionals	Kids from 3 years old Adults Teachers
7	ILA Vietnam	https://ila.edu.vn/	N/A	46	English for young learners English for adults English for corporate communication ILA Maths ILA OSC English Overseas Summer	Kids from 3 years old Adults

Interestingly, comments from the group of independent teachers who started their businesses from virtually no financial sources suggested the possibilities for individuals without resource constraints to accessing the entrepreneurial opportunities in this market with the help of technologies in Industry 4.0. This is consistent with the idea that in this era of computational entrepreneurship, entrepreneurs who have expertise in this field can have a more comfortable and cheaper way to realize their opportunities (Vuong 2019). This insight helps to shed light on the current trends of many individuals who face financial source constraints, yet still established and developed their businesses successfully in the ELTM in Vietnam. One may say that Industry 4.0 has brought about opportunities that may never have existed in the past so that entrepreneurs from any corner of the world can gain access to a broad base of customers and persuade these customers to buy their products or services.

On the other hand, participants' comments showed that except for edtech companies, technology does not change the funding sources of ELTM. Instead, it helps businesses to acquire customers and grow market share, which in turn supports the access to sources of finance. In other words, regarding entrepreneurial finance, amid Industry 4.0, start-ups in ELTM in Vietnam mostly begin with private sources of funding and, through the development process, self-fund their businesses. Only firms seeking expansion of scale, such as opening a chain of centers or rapidly penetrating the market with their education technologies, may ask for external financial sources.

These findings are in line with previous works about the financing issues of Vietnamese entrepreneurial firms. Nguyen et al. (2015) commented that the majority of SMEs are micro-enterprises with limited access to resources, such as advanced technology and formal credit (Nguyen et al. 2015). Despite their significant contributions to social and economic development, SMEs are often regarded as "the missing middle"—they are usually not the subject of interest for commercial banks. At the same time, their loans might be too large to borrow from microfinance institutions. Therefore, the most critical factor that impedes the performance of SMEs in Vietnam is the lack of capital. The authors further indicated that firms in the service sector have a lower probability of borrowing by 9% compared to industry and trade (Nguyen et al. 2015). In the ELTM market, this may be due to the fact that tangible assets, namely facilities such as classroom equipment, tables, and chairs, etc., are not the most critical resource of the firms operating in this market. The most valuable assets are intangible, including intellectual property such as the self-made syllabus or textbooks, as well as the high-quality human resource of dedicated and qualified teachers.

In another study focusing on microenterprises in Vietnam, Thai and Ngoc (2010) found out that most microentrepreneurs have to reply to their savings, partner's contributions, and borrowing from their family and friends to fund their business (Thai and Ngoc 2010). Most of them do not get funding from financial institutions. Even in the case of obtaining bank loans, these amounts could cover merely a small part of the investment needed to realize their business ideas (Thai and Ngoc 2010). These findings are similar to what is happening in the ELTM market. It again confirms the idea that, even with the rapid development of the economic and technological landscape, entrepreneurial activities in general barely benefit from additional sources of funding. The traditional finance sources which mostly come from personal resources still dominate. These call for more vigorous actions from the government policies to promote and support entrepreneurs, so that start-ups can develop more strongly in the fast-growing economy.

However, the study's results also point out the distinct characteristics of the ELTM that may influence these financing issues. English training services usually collect revenues from customers before delivering their classes. The initial investment for facilities is also rather modest compared to other start-up businesses. This is of advantage for entrepreneurs in this area and helps significantly reduce the financial barriers.

5.2. Implications

This paper suggests important implications for policymakers and entrepreneurs, as well as investors. The insights from the study can help contribute to policy formation and implementation amid Industry 4.0. Policymakers can have an overview of the technological impacts on ELTM, thereby developing appropriate legal frameworks to support the development of newly emerged market segments, especially those with a high level of technology applications. The entrepreneurial financing options and trends discussed can also provide input for the development of these frameworks. It is recommended that the authorities plan and implement more supportive policies, especially in terms of requirements and access to financing sources, such as loan banks, so as to encourage and promote entrepreneurship in the country.

For entrepreneurs and investors, the study reveals valuable insights, so that these stakeholders can evaluate investment opportunities in the field, more effectively regarding the influences of Industry 4.0. Different options of entrepreneurial finance were also discussed, which help provide input for business plans or investment decisions, which may lead to a higher chance of success in these initiatives.

6. Limitations and Future Research Directions

Despite the contribution, we fully acknowledge the limitations of this paper. Firstly, because of the nature of exploratory research, we are faced with a shortage of backing in the extant literature. Besides, with qualitative research design, the results of this study cannot be generalized to the broader populations. Due to the limited number of researchers in the education field who understand the situation of ELTM in Vietnam, the mix of participants is somewhat uneven, which may cause a biased view towards the matters of interest. The market situation of ELTM in Vietnam also keeps changing rapidly at the time of writing, with new trends and new enterprises, as well as the bankruptcy of existing firms, especially during the COVID-19 pandemic.

We understand that exploratory qualitative work has limited scientific validity, so, in the future, a more rigorous quantitative research design may be conducted to provide such validity. Researchers may also consider adopting theories or frameworks regarding technological application or adoption, to investigate, in more detail, the changing nature of the ELTM in Vietnam. Business models of typical firms in the ELTM can also be analyzed to observe the impacts of technology on financial management, as well as other business components and their outcomes. Last but not least, quantitative research design with statistical analysis should be employed to test a different hypothesis about the market and the potential entrepreneurial opportunities.

Author Contributions: Conceptualization, T.-H.P., M.-T.H., and Q.-H.V.; Data curation, T.-H.P. and M.-C.N.; Formal analysis, T.H.P., M.-C.N. and Q.H.V.; Investigation, T.-H.P.; Methodology, T.-H.P., M.-T.H. and T.-T.V.; Project administration, T.-H.P., M.-T.H. and M.-C.N.; Supervision, Q.-H.V.; Writing—original draft, T.-H.P.; Writing—review and editing, M.-T.H., T.-T.V. and Q.-H.V. All authors have read and agreed to the published version of the manuscript.

Funding: This research received no external funding.

Conflicts of Interest: The authors declare no conflict of interest.

Appendix A

Table A1. Profile of participants.

Participant Number	Researcher/Entrepreneur	Gender and Age Bracket in Years	Details
1	Researcher	Male 35–39	More than 20 peer-reviewed articles in international books and journals as well as multiple reports and conference papers written in Vietnamese and English for scholarly audiences globally
2	Researcher	Male 30–34	Seven peer-reviewed articles in international books and journals as well as multiple reports and conference papers written in Vietnamese and English for scholarly audiences globally
3	Entrepreneur	Female 35–39	An English language training center established from 2009 with more than 3000 learners, currently focusing on primary and secondary students, applying blended learning from 2015
4	Entrepreneur	Female 35–39	An English language training center established from 2017 with a total of around 2000 learners, focusing on training job readiness for university students together with English skills
5	Entrepreneur	Male 30–34	An English language training center from 2017 located in suburban areas of Hanoi with 700 students studying in the center now.
6	Entrepreneur	Male 35–39	Applications to support learning foreign languages for kids 0–10 years old
7	Entrepreneur	Male 30–34	An independent English instructor who operates small-sized classes, focusing on IELTS test preparation in both online and offline modes
8	Entrepreneur	Female 30–34	A university lecturer who started an English language training center from 2012 with small-sized classes for kids and teenagers
9	Entrepreneur	Female 30–34	An independent English instructor who is currently in the United States and runs online classes, focusing on IELTS test preparation and communicative English
10	Entrepreneur	Female 40–44	An English language training center franchised from 2015, providing services both to the center's customers as well as to public-owned schools
11	Entrepreneur	Female 25–29	An independent English instructor started teaching from 2016 and had more than 1000 students, focusing on IELTS test preparation
12	Entrepreneur	Male 30–35	An English language training center established in 2012 with services ranging from providing training courses to corporations to cooperating with public-owned schools and teaching students at the center.

References

Ahlstrom, David. 2010. Innovation and growth: How business contributes to society. *Academy of Management Perspectives* 24: 11–24.

Ahlstrom, David, Amber Y. Chang, and Jessie S. T. Cheung. 2019. Encouraging entrepreneurship and economic growth. *Journal of Risk and Financial Management* 12: 178. [CrossRef]

Andersen, Steffen, and Kasper Meisner Nielsen. 2012. Ability or finances as constraints on entrepreneurship? evidence from survival rates in a natural experiment. *The Review of Financial Studies* 25: 3684–710. [CrossRef]

Anh, Huong. 2020. Mastering Technology for Vietnam's Growth. Available online: https://www.vir.com.vn/mastering-technology-for-vietnams-growth-67693.html (accessed on 24 February 2020).

ANT Consulting. 2020. The Middle Class of Vietnam Increased Sharply. Available online: http://www.antconsult.vn/news/the-middle-class-of-vietnam-increased-sharply.html#ixzz6E6kFi9uG (accessed on 24 February 2020).

Banister, Peter. 2011. *Qualitative Methods in Psychology: A Research Guide*. New York: McGraw-Hill Education.

Bellavitis, Cristiano, Igor Filatotchev, Dzidziso Samuel Kamuriwo, and Tom Vanacker. 2017. Entrepreneurial finance: New frontiers of research and practice. *Venture Capital* 19: 1–16. [CrossRef]

Belleflamme, Paul, Thomas Lambert, and Armin Schwienbacher. 2014. Crowdfunding: Tapping the right crowd. *Journal of Business Venturing* 29: 585–609. [CrossRef]

Berger, Allen N., and Gregory F. Udell. 1998. The economics of small business finance: The roles of private equity and debt markets in the financial growth cycle. *Journal of Banking & Finance* 22: 613–73. [CrossRef]

BMI. 2019. Education in Vietnam. Available online: https://bmiglobaled.com/Market-Reports/Vietnam/education (accessed on 12 May 2020).

Bradley, Wendy A., Gilles Duruflé, Thomas. F. Hellmann, and Karen E. Wilson. 2019. Cross-border venture capital investments: What is the role of public policy? *Journal of Risk and Financial Management* 12: 112. [CrossRef]

British Business Group Vietnam. 2018. *Vietnam—2018 Education*. Hanoi: British Business Group Vietnam.

Bui, Thuy Thi Ngoc, and Hoa Thi Mai Nguyen. 2016. Standardizing english for educational and socio-economic betterment-a critical analysis of english language policy reforms in Vietnam. In *English Language Education Policy in Asia*. New York: Springer, pp. 363–88.

Cassar, Gavin. 2004. The financing of business start-ups. *Journal of Business Venturing* 19: 261–83. [CrossRef]

Cavaco, Afonso. M., J. P. Sousa Dias, and Ian P. Bates. 2005. Consumers' perceptions of community pharmacy in Portugal: A qualitative exploratory study. *Pharmacy World and Science* 27: 54–60. [CrossRef]

Central Intelligence Agency. 2020. The World Factbook Vietnam. Available online: https://www.cia.gov/library/publications/resources/the-world-factbook/ (accessed on 24 February 2020).

Charlton, Gina S., and Corinne J. Barrow. 2002. Coping and self-help group membership in Parkinson's disease: An exploratory qualitative study. *Health & Social Care in the Community* 10: 472–78.

Cole, Rebel A., and Tatyana Sokolyk. 2018. Debt financing, survival, and growth of start-up firms. *Journal of Corporate Finance* 50: 609–25. [CrossRef]

Tech Collective. 2019. Vietnam's Emerging Edtech Startups. Available online: https://techcollectivesea.com/2019/12/03/vietnams-emerging-edtech-startups/ (accessed on 23 April 2019).

Cumming, Douglas, and Alexander Peter Groh. 2018. Entrepreneurial finance: Unifying themes and future directions. *Journal of Corporate Finance* 50: 538–55. [CrossRef]

De Bettignies, Jean-Etienne, and James A. Brander. 2007. Financing entrepreneurship: Bank finance versus venture capital. *Journal of Business Venturing* 22: 808–32. [CrossRef]

Denis, David J. 2004. Entrepreneurial finance: An overview of the issues and evidence. *Journal of Corporate Finance* 10: 301–26. [CrossRef]

Department of Education and Training Hanoi. 2018. List of Licensed Foreign Language and Informatics Centers. Available online: http://sogd.hanoi.gov.vn/trung-tam-ngoai-nha-truong/danh-sach-cac-trung-tam-ngoai-ngu-tinh-den-ngay-30122018-cm1099-6896.aspx (accessed on 22 March 2020).

Department of Education and Training Hanoi. 2019. List of Licensed Foreign Language and Informatics Centers. Available online: http://sogd.hanoi.gov.vn/trung-tam-ngoai-truong/danh-sach-cac-trung-tam-ngoai-ngu-tin-hoc-tinh-den-31122019-tren-dia-ban-thanh-c1099-9851.aspx (accessed on 22 March 2020).

Department of Education and Training. 2017. List of Licensed Foreign Language and Informatics Centers. Available online: https://hcm.edu.vn/thong-bao/danh-sach-cac-trung-tam-ngoai-ngu-tin-hoc-da-duoc-cap-phep-tinh-den-ngay-12-tha-cmobile41012-57342.aspx (accessed on 22 March 2020).

Department of Education and Training. 2019. List of Licensed Foreign Language and Informatics Centers. Available online: http://edu.hochiminhcity.gov.vn/chuyen-muc/danh-sach-cac-trung-tam-ngoai-ngu-tin-hoc-duoc-cap-phep-cap-nhat-den-ngay-12032-cmobile41743-61861.aspx (accessed on 22 March 2020).

Education First. 2019. *EF English Proficiency Index*, 9th ed. Lucerne: Education First.

Lincoln, Yvonna S., and Egon G. Guba. 1985. *Naturalistic Inquiry*. Beverley Hills: Sage.

EVBN. 2018. *Education in Vietnam Edition 2018*. Ho Chi Minh City, Vietnam: EU-Vietnam Business Network.

Horák, Josef. 2016. Does Industry 4.0 Influence Efficiency of Financial Management of a Company. *Pargue: The 10th International Days of Statistics and Economics*. Available online: https://msed.vse.cz/msed_2016/article/174-Horak-Josef-paper.pdf (accessed on 12 May 2020).

Huyghebaert, Nancy, and Linda M. Van de Gucht. 2007. The Determinants of Financial Structure: New Insights from Business Start-ups. *European Financial Management* 13: 101–33. [CrossRef]

La, Viet-Phuong, and Quan-Hoang Vuong. 2019. *Bayesvl: Visually Learning the Graphical Structure of Bayesian Networks and Performing MCMC with 'Stan'*; The Comprehensive R Archive Network (CRAN). Available online: https://cran.r-project.org/web/packages/bayesvl/index.html (accessed on 12 May 2020).

La, Viet-Phuong, Thanh-Hang Pham, Manh-Toan Ho, Minh-Hoang Nguyen, Khanh-Linh P. Nguyen, Thu-Trang Vuong, Hong-Kong T. Nguyen, Trung Tran, Quy Khuc, Manh-Tung Ho, and et al. 2020. Policy Response, Social Media and Science Journalism for the Sustainability of the Public Health System Amid the COVID-19 Outbreak: The Vietnam Lessons. *Sustainability* 12: 2931. [CrossRef]

Le, Viet, Xuan-Binh Vu, and Son Nghiem. 2018. Technical efficiency of small and medium manufacturing firms in Vietnam: A stochastic meta-frontier analysis. *Economic Analysis and Policy* 59: 84–91. [CrossRef]

Le, Van Huy, Frantz Rowe, Duane Truex, and Minh Q. Huynh. 2012. An empirical study of determinants of e-commerce adoption in SMEs in Vietnam: An economy in transition. *Journal of Global Information Management* 20: 23–54. [CrossRef]

McKinsey & Company. 2019. Seizing the Fast-Growing Retail Opportunity in Vietnam. Available online: https://www.mckinsey.com/~{}/media/mckinsey/industries/retail/our%20insights/how%20companies%20can%20seize%20opportunity%20in%20vietnams%20growing%20retail%20market/seizing-the-fast-growing-retail-opportunity-in-vietnam.ashx (accessed on 24 April 2020).

Meyer, M., D. Libaers, B. Thijs, K. Grant, W. Glänzel, and K. Debackere. 2014. Origin and emergence of entrepreneurship as a research field. *Scientometrics* 98: 473–85. [CrossRef]

Miglo, Anton. 2020. Crowdfunding in a Competitive Environment. *Journal of Risk and Financial Management* 13: 39. [CrossRef]

Nguyen, Thi Bich Ngoc. 2019. Kaizen PE Strikes First Deal in Vietnam, Invests $10m in YOLA. Available online: https://www.dealstreetasia.com/stories/kaizen-pe-yola-147120/ (accessed on 22 April 2020).

Nguyen, Ha. 2020. Total Workforce Index 2019—3 Challenges for Vietnam's Labor. Available online: https://www.vietnam-briefing.com/news/total-workforce-index-2019-3-challenges-vietnams-labor.html/ (accessed on 24 February 2020).

Nguyen, Thi Nhung, Christopher Gan, and Baiding Hu. 2015. An Empirical Analysis of Credit Accessibilty of Small and Medium Sized Enterprises in Vietnam. *Banks and Bank System* 10: 34–46.

Nhung, Hong. 2020. Apax Holdings Lists on HoSE. Available online: http://vneconomictimes.com/article/banking-finance/apax-holdings-lists-on-hose (accessed on 26 April 2020).

Paré, Jean-Louis, Jean Rédis, and Jean-Michel Sahut. 2009. The development of entrepreneurial finance research. *International Journal of Business* 14: 283.

Phan, Nghia. 2019. Vietnam's English Proficiency Drops in 2019 Ranking. Vnexpress International. Available online: https://e.vnexpress.net/news/news/vietnam-s-english-proficiency-drops-in-2019-ranking-4008398.html (accessed on 12 May 2020).

Kvale, Steinar. 1996. *Interviews: An Introduction to Qualitative Research Interviewing*. Thousand Oaks: Sage.

Prime Minister. 2001. Directive No.14/2001/CT-TTg, Promulgated by the Prime Minister of Government, on Renovation of the General Education Program in Execution of Resolution No. 40/2000/QH10 of the National Assembly. Available online: https://thuvienphapluat.vn/van-ban/giao-duc/Chi-thi-14-2001-CT-TTg-doi-moi-chuong-trinh-giao-duc-pho-thong-thuc-hien-Nghi-quyet-40-2000-QH10-47782.aspx (accessed on 12 May 2020).

Quinn Patton, Michael. 2002. *Qualitative Research and Evaluation Methods*. Thousand Oaks: Sage.

Robson, Colin. 2002. *Real World Research: A Resource for Social Scientists and Practitioner-Researchers*. Oxford: Blackwell Oxford, vol. 2.

Russell, Jon. 2018. Topica raises $50M for its online learning services in Southeast Asia. Available online: https://techcrunch.com/2018/11/27/topica-raises-50m/ (accessed on 23 April 2020).

Russell, Jon. 2019. Gradient Ventures, Google's AI Fund, Leads $7M Investment in English Learning app Elsa. Available online: https://techcrunch.com/2019/02/26/gradient-ventures-elsa-7-million/ (accessed on 22 April 2020).

Santarelli, Enrico, and Hien Thu Tran. 2013. The interplay of human and social capital in shaping entrepreneurial performance: The case of Vietnam. *Small Business Economics* 40: 435–58. [CrossRef]

Shane, Scott Andrew. 2003. *A General Theory of Entrepreneurship: The Individual-Opportunity Nexus*. Cheltenham: Edward Elgar Publishing.

Shane, Scott, and S. Venkataraman. 2000. The promise of entrepreneurship as a field of research. *Academy of Management Review* 25: 217–26. [CrossRef]

Spradley, James P. 2016. *Participant Observation*. Long Grove: Waveland Press.

Thai, Mai Thi Thanh, and Ho Thuy Ngoc. 2010. Microentrepreneurship in a transitional economy: Evidence from Vietnam. In *Contemporary Micro-Enterprise: Concepts and Cases*. Cheltenham: Edward Elgar, pp. 32–48.

Thao, Hoang Thi Phuong, and Fredric William Swierczek. 2008. Internet use, customer relationships and loyalty in the Vietnamese travel industry. *Asia Pacific Journal of Marketing and Logistics* 20: 190–210. [CrossRef]

The World Bank Vietnam. 2020. Vietnam Overview. Available online: https://www.worldbank.org/en/country/vietnam/overview (accessed on 24 February 2020).

The World Bank. 2020. Theoretical Framework. Available online: https://data.worldbank.org/indicator/BX.KLT.DINV.CD.WD (accessed on 25 April 2020).

Tipu, Syed Awais Ahmad, and Faisal Manzoor Arain. 2011. Managing success factors in entrepreneurial ventures: A behavioral approach. *International Journal of Entrepreneurial Behavior & Research* 17: 534–60.

Trines, Stefan. Education in Vietnam. Available online: https://wenr.wes.org/2017/11/education-in-vietnam (accessed on 24 February 2020).

Tuoi Tre News. 2019. English proficiency of Vietnamese hits five-year low: EF report. *Tuoi Tre News*, November 6.

UNESCO Institute of Statistics. 2020. Education: Outbound Internationally Mobile Students by Host Region. Available online: http://data.uis.unesco.org/Index.aspx?queryid=172 (accessed on 27 February 2020).

Urbano, David, Sebastian Aparicio, and David Audretsch. 2019. Twenty-five years of research on institutions, entrepreneurship, and economic growth: What has been learned? *Small Business Economics* 53: 21–49. [CrossRef]

Vanham, Peter. 2018. The Story of Viet Nam's Economic Miracle. Available online: https://www.weforum.org/agenda/2018/09/how-vietnam-became-an-economic-miracle/ (accessed on 26 February 2020).

Venkataraman, S. 1997. The Distinctive Domain of Entrepreneurship Research. In *Advances in Entrepreneurship, Firm Emergence, and Growth*. Edited by Jerome Katz and R Brockhaus. Greenwich: JAI Press, pp. 119–38.

Viet Nam News. 2018. PM Pledges to Realise Industry 4.0 Opportunities. Available online: https://vietnamnews.vn/economy/451777/pm-pledges-to-realise-industry-40-opportunities.html#rSRPJ6mkrhiQ6qA9.99 (accessed on 25 April 2020).

Vietnam Economic Times. 2020. Key Requirement. Available online: http://vneconomictimes.com/article/vietnam-today/key-requirement (accessed on 27 March 2020).

Vuong, Quan Hoang. 2016. Impacts of geographical locations and sociocultural traits on the Vietnamese entrepreneurship. *SpringerPlus* 5: 1189. [CrossRef]

Vuong, Quan-Hoang. 2019. Computational entrepreneurship: From economic complexities to interdisciplinary research. *Business Perspectives* 17: 117–29. [CrossRef]

Vuong, Quan Hoang, and Nancy. K. Napier. 2015. Acculturation and global mindsponge: An emerging market perspective. *International Journal of Intercultural Relations* 49: 354–67. [CrossRef]

Vuong, Quan-Hoang, Quang-Khiem Bui, Viet-Phuong La, Thu-Trang Vuong, Viet-Ha T. Nguyen, Manh-Toan Ho, Hong-Kong T. Nguyen, and Manh-Tung Ho. 2018. Cultural additivity: Behavioural insights from the interaction of Confucianism, Buddhism and Taoism in folktales. *Palgrave Communications* 4: 143. [CrossRef]

Vuong, Quan-Hoang, Thi-Hanh Vu, Quang-Hung Doan, and Manh-Tung Ho. 2019. Determinants of Vietnamese footwear exporting firms' market selection: A multinomial logistic analysis of panel data. *Heliyon* 5: e02582. [CrossRef] [PubMed]

Vuong, Quan-Hoang, Viet-Phuong La, Thu-Trang Vuong, Hong-Kong T. Nguyen, Manh-Tung Ho, and Manh-Toan Ho. 2020. What have Vietnamese scholars learned from researching entrepreneurship? A Systematic review. *Heliyon* 6. [CrossRef] [PubMed]

Vuong, Quan-Hoang, Viet-Phuong La, Thu-Trang Vuong, Phuong Hanh Hoang, Manh Toan Ho, Manh Tung Ho, and Hong Kong T. Nguyen. 2020. Multi-faceted insights of entrepreneurship facing a fast-growing economy: A literature review. *Open Economics* 3: 25–41. [CrossRef]

Vuong, Quan-Hoang, Manh-Tung Ho, Hong-Kong T. Nguyen, Thu-Trang Vuong, Trung Tran, Khanh-Linh Hoang, Thi-Hanh Vu, Phuong-Hanh Hoang, Minh-Hoang Nguyen, Manh-Toan Ho, and et al. 2020. On how religions could accidentally incite lies and violence: Folktales as a cultural transmitter. *Palgrave Communications* 6: 82. [CrossRef]

Vuong, Quan-Hoang, La Viet-Phuong, Nguyen Minh-Hoang, Ho Manh-Toan, Ho Manh-Tung, and Peter Mantello. 2020. Improving Bayesian statistics understanding in the age of Big Data with the bayesvl R package. *Software Impacts* 4: 100016. [CrossRef]

World Bank Group. 2016. *Vietnam 2035 Toward Prosperity, Creativity, Equity, and Democracy*. Washington, DC: World Bank Group, Available online: http://hdl.handle.net/10986/23724 (accessed on 12 May 2020).

World Economic Forum. 2020. The Story of Viet Nam's Economic Miracle. Available online: https://www.weforum.org/agenda/2018/09/how-vietnam-became-an-economic-miracle/ (accessed on 26 April 2020).

Zarutskie, Rebecca. 2006. Evidence on the effects of bank competition on firm borrowing and investment. *Journal of Financial Economics* 81: 503–37. [CrossRef]

© 2020 by the authors. Licensee MDPI, Basel, Switzerland. This article is an open access article distributed under the terms and conditions of the Creative Commons Attribution (CC BY) license (http://creativecommons.org/licenses/by/4.0/).

Article

Evidence of the Environmental Kuznets Curve: Unleashing the Opportunity of Industry 4.0 in Emerging Economies

Viktoriia Koilo

Hauge School of Management, NLA University College, Linstows gate 3, Oslo 0130, Norway; viktoriia.koilo@nla.no

Received: 4 July 2019; Accepted: 18 July 2019; Published: 20 July 2019

Abstract: This study aims to investigate the relationship of economic development, measured as economic growth, energy use, trade and foreign direct investment, on the one hand, and environmental degradation (carbon dioxide (hereafter CO_2) emissions), on the other hand, in eleven emerging Eastern European and Central Asian countries during the period of 1990 to 2014. The empirical results give an evidence of a carbon emission Kuznets curve for these emerging economies. The current income level indicates that not every country has reached the turning point for CO_2 emissions reductions. Income elasticities for CO_2 are positive for all eleven countries. The paper concludes that within the group, Ukraine and Kazakhstan have the most sensitive change in economic growth in respect to CO_2. In addition, it concludes that there is a negative effect of total energy consumption on environment as such consumption increases CO_2 emissions. The results also show a positive effect of foreign direct investment (FDI) on CO_2 emissions in Eastern European and Central Asian countries. It is expected that the innovative transition to a low-carbon economy offers great opportunities for economic growth and job creation. Technological leadership (the initiative Industry 4.0) should be accompanied by the development and introduction of new technologies throughout Eastern European and Central Asian countries, hence, the paradigm of "sustainable development" should be considered as fatal. Furthermore, Eastern European and Central Asian economies should consider the experience of policy making implications made by other developing countries in gaining sustainable growth. Econometric analyses prove the existence of different impact on energy consumption of the ICT sector, which plays a key supporting role for intelligent manufacturing. Thus, there is a need for further investigations of the relationship between technology use and CO_2 emissions.

Keywords: environmental Kuznets curve (EKC); Industry 4.0; information and communications technology (ICT); wave of environmentalism; energy intensive industry; income elasticity of CO_2; U-shaped relationship

1. Introduction

In time of global climate change and risks it poses, a question arises: "Why is it vital for global security and stability to tackle climate change and invest in sustainability?". According to the report of the World Wide Fund for Nature, there is a statement concerning the 3S doctrine. It can be summed up in the following formula: a system that is not environmentally sustainable creates instability that inevitably devolves into insecurity. In other words: an environmentally unsustainable system produces instability, which leads to insecurity. When the balance between man and the ecosystem that provides him with key resources is upset, instability takes over; and in areas unprepared for these situations, the threats to security and economic growth arise as well (WWF 2017).

Figure 1 presents a vision of the relationship between sustainable development and key economic components.

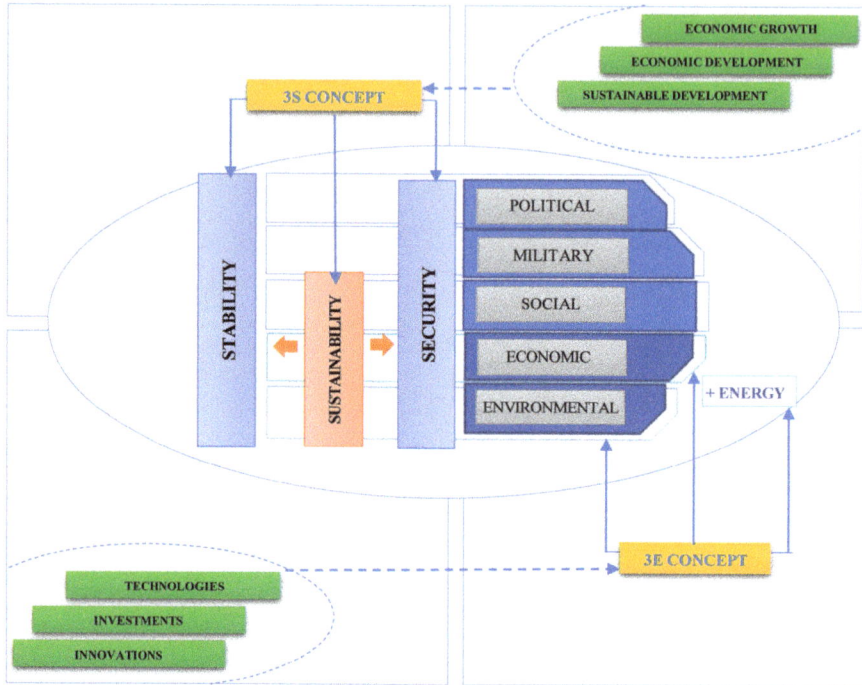

Figure 1. The relationship between sustainable development and key economic components. Source: Compiled by author.

From Figure 1 we can see that the sustainable development paradigm is based on three main pillars: environmental protection, social justice, and economic development. In recent studies researches consider such development as a complex of strong ethical and moral goals as what should be done. Such a pronouncement is called a moral imperative and it incorporates three main elements: satisfying human needs, ensuring social equity and respecting environmental limits (Holden et al. 2017).

If the system is not stable it cannot be resistant to changes, and—thus, not able to sustain values in future. This may lead to an increase of threats to the security in unprepared areas. In other words, there should be an economy, which is able to meet the needs of society and express potentials at present, while preserving biodiversity and natural ecosystems for future generations. Furthermore, in a world where security is of ever-greater importance, relevant parameters should be taken into account to analyze problems and come up with the most effective responses. The first requirement is to recognize that climate changes and the risks they pose are a threat to stability and security. It should be noted that in some national classifications energy is used as a part of economic security (Buzan et al. 1998). But in fact, energy security is more about the link between national security and availability of natural resources for energy consumption. Hence, economic, environmental, and energy securities together create the 3E-concept.

In the market it is important to find the cheapest ways of energy resources' supply. This issue disturbs lots of countries and creates many threats to national security and sustainable development.

It is not easy to build sustainable system and at the same time continue to increase production capacity of the country Moreover, economic growth is finally entering a new era of automation and data exchange in manufacturing technologies (Industry 4.0) that is driven by the interaction between sustainable infrastructure investment, resource productivity and rapid technological innovation.

On entering into Industry 4.0, one is faced with the 4th Wave of Environmentalism, which is characterized by the use of innovation, digital technologies, and achievement of different environmental goals, such as reduction of natural resource consumption, CO2 emissions and waste generation (Manoukian 2018). In "Business and the Fourth Wave of Environmentalism" by Environmental Defense Fund (2018) it is stated that there are several technologies which can drive sustainability: data analytics, block-chain, automation technologies, sharing technologies, sensors, dematerialization, and mobile ubiquity.

Obviously, innovations can speed the transition to a low-carbon economy and create smart traffic management networks, which allow use of less energy and propose better ways to conserve fuel resources. However, several questions arise: is society prepared to deal with the environmental challenges and does Industry 4.0 affect the environmental sustainability in emerging economies?

Thus, there is a need to investigate the relationship between economic development and environmental degradation in emerging economies, and the expected profound impact of Industry 4.0 on emerging economies.

Without doubt, the inherent characteristics of new technologies make an impact on energy, flow of raw materials, waste, etc. and these changes have an influence on environmental sustainability. It is expected that there should be a synergy effect between Industry 4.0 and sustainability. The setting of goals is an important condition to begin the journey towards sustainability (Bonilla et al. 2018).

According to the Paris Climate Agreement and the United Nations Program 2015, in order to meet the Sustainable Development Goals (SDGs) it is necessary to create an integrated environmental performance methodology to investigate countries' pollution situation and measure the deterioration of natural resources. For this purpose, a new approach was presented, which calculated the Environmental Performance Index (EPI).

EPI scores 180 countries on 24 performance indicators across ten issue categories covering environmental health and ecosystem vitality.

The evaluation of environmental situation is better to do in comparison with the level of economic development of the countries. Therefore, it was decided to present this relationship between EPI and Human Development Index (HDI) in form of the correlation matrix. The analysis shows the situation in Eastern European and Central Asian countries and compared them with TOP-11 developed countries.

As can be seen from the Figure 2 for emerging economies the EPI varies from 0.26 to 0.70 and for developed economies from 0.48 to 0.90 respectively.

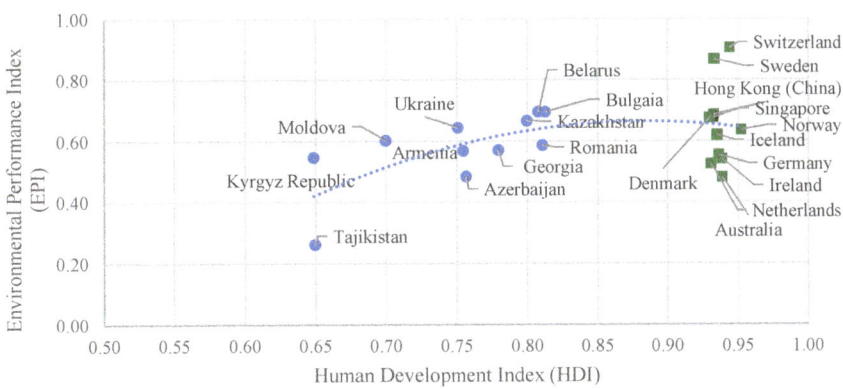

Figure 2. Correlation matrix between the Environmental Performance Index (EPI-2018) and the Human Development Index (HDI-2017). Sources: The Environmental Performance Index (2018) and Human Development Index (2017).

The HDI is different for these groups, as emerging economies are classified as countries with high human development and developed economies with very high human development. Nevertheless, the environmental pollution levels do not show a significant difference.

It should be noted that energy use and economic development could be important sources of variation in CO2 emissions for economies characterized by a rapid increase in economic activity and at the same time characterized by obsolete machinery and equipment. These economies have both energy-intensive production and high levels of CO2 emissions.

Hence, studying the relationship between environmental degradation, economic development, and energy use is an important issue for research.

2. Theoretical Background

2.1. Studies on the Relationship between the Economic Development and Environmental Degradation

Issues concerning relationships between environmental indicators and income have been widely discussed. A major concept is investigation of the environmental Kuznets curve (EKC) hypothesis, which refers to the inverted U-shaped curve, mapping the relationship between economic growth and environmental degradation.

The original EKC hypothesis suggests that while improving economic development the environment at the initial stage is rapidly deteriorating. However, along with increase of income, demand for a safe and prosperous environment grows (Stern 2004).

In the work of Frankel and Rose (2005) the EKC analysis was extended by adding new variable—trade liberalization. Empirical testing proved the EKC hypothesis and also indicated a positive influence of trade on environmental pollution.

Similarly, the influence of economic growth, FDI inflows and trade on CO2 emissions was investigated in Turkey (Kaya et al. 2017). The authors found empirical evidence of the existence of the EKC in this country and positive long run effects of variables on CO2 emissions.

Another approach presented by Kacar and Kayalica (2014): examined the relationship between sulfur emission and economic development. Again, one found evidence of the EKC hypothesis.

A recent study investigated the long-run relationship between CO2 emissions, economic growth and energy use in North Africa and the Middle East (Zaied et al. 2017). In their study it was concluded that only oil producing countries have already reached the inflection turning point of emissions.

Tjoek and Wu (2018) analyzed the relationship between SO2 and CO2 emissions and economic growth. The results showed that the EKC hypotheses can be applied for CO2 emissions. They also argued that the current Southeast Asia income level has not reached the inflection turning point.

In a study Shahbaz and Sinha (2018) states that developing and emerging economies still have not reached the turning point, but it is possible to do so in sustainable manner ensuring an inclusive growth. Thus, an approach, which is based on public-private partnership, should be considered.

Panayotou (1993) empirically examined and made a policy analysis of environmental degradation at different stages of economic development. He established that environmental degradation is worse in countries with income per capita levels less than $1000. Another group of countries ($1000–$3000) is characterized by a transition tendency from agricultural to industrial economy. The last group ($10,000) shows a shift from energy intensive manufacturing to information/technology-intensive production.

Blunck and Werthmann (2019) tested if green growth policies can help to protect the environment and keep the industrial growth at the same time. The final estimation showed a mixed evidence for the EKC hypothesis.

2.2. Concept of Industry 4.0 and Sustainability Implications

The term "Industry 4.0" was introduced in 2011, when the business community of German political and academic circles launched an initiative under this name to increase the competitiveness of German industry (Kagermann et al. 2011). Additionally, it was mentioned that the fourth Industrial Revolution (Industry 4.0) proposes intelligent manufacturing through development of Cyber-Physical Production

Systems (CPPS), equipped with large variety of digital technologies. These systems include objectives communicating with each other, and exchange with autonomous and self-optimized information. Hence CPPS rely on further implementation of computer, manufacturing science and technology, along with ICT (Kagermann et al. 2013).

It should be mentioned that Industry 4—is not just about helping people to minimize and eliminate problems, but also about innovations, increase of productivity and more customer-centricity (Lee et al. 2018).

Industrial enterprises around the world are beginning to pay attention to business in the context of the Industry 4.0 program. About a third of companies all over the world estimate their level of digitalization as high. In the next five years, the share of such companies is expected to increase from 33% to 72%. For example, according to forecasts, it is expected that the number of connected devices will exceed 30 billion in the next few years (PricewaterhouseCoopers 2016). Hence, there is a growing trend in ICT demand.

Also, it should be noted that one of the most important aspects of implementation of Industry 4.0 are the rational use of natural resources and energy efficient technologies (Blunck and Werthmann 2017). In this regard Industry 4.0 was also discussed in relation to the SDGs (Figure 3).

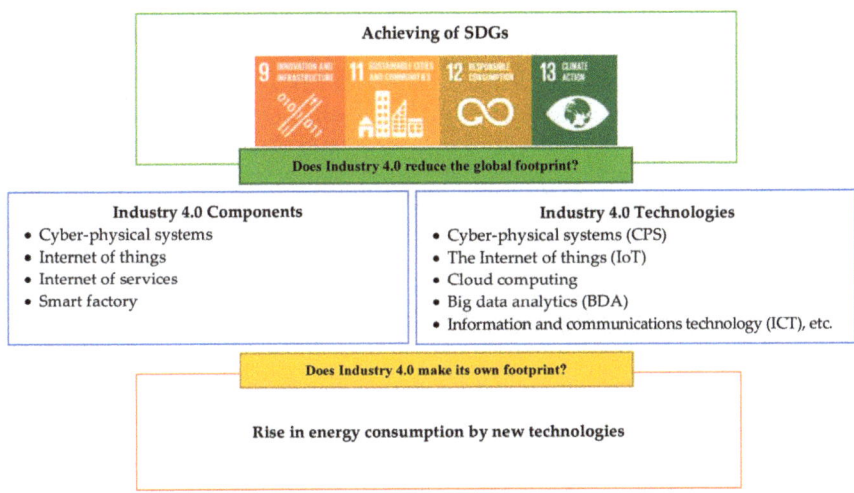

Figure 3. Concept of Industry 4.0 and sustainability implications. Source: Compiled by author.

For example, for achieving SDG #9 new technologies can contribute to the integration of renewable energy sources and digitization of production processes.

SDG #11—Industry 4.0 provides an opportunity to explore the potential of cities, apply innovative development, digitalization and new technologies, especially information and communication technologies (ICTs).

SDG #12—ICTs can also contribute to sustainable consumption and production, and also be useful for improving resource utilization (The Division for Sustainable Development Goals DSDG).

Nonetheless, Industry 4.0, especially ICT, can have different impact on sustainability, both positive and critical.

In fact, the ICT sector consumes 7% of the world electricity, and the share is expected to rise approximately to 13% in ten years (Bertoldi et al. 2017). Moreover, the rapid growth of new data centers has fastened the carbon footprint increase. Literature review shows that this issue has been widely discussed. The impact and problems of Industry 4.0 on sustainability have been studied in four different scenarios: deployment, operation and technology, integration, and compliance with sustainable development goals and long-term scenarios (Bonilla et al. 2018).

Despite the fact that information and communication technologies are responsible only for about 2% of anthropogenic emissions ICT is one of the fastest growing sectors of the economy. As result, there is growing concern about the impact of the sector on the environment, especially on the potential climate change caused by related energy consumption. At the same time, there is a growing understanding that ICTs can also significantly reduce the environmental impact of other sectors, by increasing their energy efficiency (Pouri and Hilty 2018).

To sum up, this study will contribute to the existing literature in two ways. Firstly, this paper will provide insights about the carbon emission Kuznets curve in Eastern European and Central Asian countries. Secondly, study will examine the impact of the ICT use on energy consumption in each region.

3. Data and Methodology

In order to test the relationship between air pollution and economic development this paper applies annual data of GDP, net inflows of FDI, energy intensity and trade openness. The data are gathered from the open World Bank database (The World Bank 2019). The indicators were assessed by national statistical authorities and then processed by the World Bank under common processing standards. It would have been preferable to use quarterly data for the analysis, but due to the lack of reliable series it is decided to use annual data, covering the years from 1990 to 2014. The average values of the indicators have been processed to a certain degree using a repeated observation method.

A Hodrick Prescott-filter is used to find significant short-term deviations from long-term equilibriums in data serials (Annen 2006). However, the results show that there are no significant deviations from trend, hence there is no need to use structural time series analysis to separate cycle component and trend.

The following study is based on the analysis of indicators of eleven Eastern European and Central Asian economies, i.e., Armenia, Azerbaijan, Belarus, Bulgaria, Georgia, Kazakhstan, Kyrgyz Republic, Moldova, Romania, Tajikistan, and Ukraine. These countries had until the 1990s approximately the same economic systems and mechanisms, and, thereafter, began to transform their political and economic systems towards market-oriented economies.

The main common characteristics for these countries a rapid growth pace of foreign trade, significant increase of the share of the private sector, and foreign investment remains key factor for economic growth. Also, the structure of the economy of the countries of Eastern Europe and Central Asia is changing. Previously the national economies of these countries were oriented to agriculture, extraction of raw materials and production of low-level processed products. Then, during the reform the share of ready-made industrial products, with high technology standards, competitive at international level, increased.

Nevertheless, for most post socialist countries the biggest serious issue for development of its own industry still is the dependence on import of energy resources at market prices. This problem is very difficult to solve due to the fact that in Soviet times, production as a whole had high energy intensity.

Thus, investigating the relationship between environmental degradation, economic development, and energy use in emerging economies is an important task.

The paper uses a logarithmic form of the variables to make differences relative and reduce the effect of heteroscedasticity problems.

It should be noted, when using econometric models based on time series, an important point is to check the adequacy of these models. Hence, the paper applies different econometric tools to proceed the regression validation. A Durbin–Watson test has been included to detect possible autocorrelation of the residuals (Hisamatsu and Maekawa 1994). An important precondition for obtaining reliable results are stationary circumstances. Therefore, it is necessary to check the model for stationary This is done by using a Dickey–Fuller test (EViews 2019).

In this paper a log-linear quadratic regression was used to check the environmental Kuznets curve hypothesis on the relationships between the explanatory variables and carbon emission:

$$logCO2_t = \alpha + \beta_1 logGDPt + \beta_2 log^2GDP_t + \beta_3 logFDI_t + \beta_4 logEnergy_t + \beta_5 logTrade_t + \varepsilon_t \qquad (1)$$

where

$logCO2_t$—is the logarithm of CO2 emissions;
$logGDP_t$ and log^2GDP_t—is the logarithm of GDP and its square;
$logFDI_t$—is the logarithm of FDI net inflows;
$logTrade_t$—is the logarithm of trade in services (the sum of service exports and imports divided by the value of GDP);
$logEnergy_t$—is the logarithm of energy intensity level of primary energy;
t—is the sampling year;
ε—is the vector of the residuals;

The foundation of the environmental Kuznets curve hypothesis is that the environmental degradation level is expected to increase at the same time as real GDP per capita increases, until a certain point, at which environmental degradation is expected to decrease as income per capita enters a different level (Xu et al. 2018). The relationship between emissions and economic growth is explained as follows:

- if $\beta_2 = \beta_1 = 0$, the hypothesis on the relationships between economic growth and environmental degradation can be rejected;
- if $\beta_2 = 0$ and $\beta_1 > 0$, there is a linear relationship;
- if $\beta_1 > 0$ and $\beta_2 < 0$, there is an inverted U-shaped relationship between economic growth and CO2 emission (in this case, the environmental Kuznets curve hypothesis can be accepted);
- if $\beta_1 < 0$ and $\beta_2 > 0$, there is a positive U-shaped relationship;

where $-\beta_1/2\beta_2$ is the inflection point.

In addition, the study examines the influence of the ICT use on energy consumption, which was based on the Statistical Review of World Energy and has been provided by BP (BP Statistical Review of World Energy 2018). ITU Telecom World presents data of the global ICT sector for the major world manufacturers, telecom operators and innovative players which are guided by new technologies (International Telecommunication Union 2017).

Among the main indicators, which characterize ICT development are: ICT1—Fixed-telephone subscriptions; ICT2—Mobile-cellular telephone subscriptions; ICT3—Individuals using the Internet. The following study is based on the analysis of indicators of six regions. The data was collected for the period 2005–2017.

It explores the relationship between energy consumption and ICT variables in Microsoft Excel using econometric analysis.

4. Results

4.1. Regressions on Relationships between Carbon Emission and Economic Development

Based on the adjusted R^2 value, it can be concluded that the model can explain 95% of the variation in CO2 emissions. In addition, the error correction term is 0.05. The results are reliable (statistically significant): Prob (F-statistic) is less than 0.05. Another step is finding the likelihood of the sample result, if the null hypothesis is true:

H_0: $\mu_1 = \mu_2 = \mu_3$
H_1: at least one of the means is different.

If F > F criteria, we reject the null hypothesis. In this case, 92.94 > 0.00 (Table 1). Hence, the null hypothesis can be rejected.

Table 1. Regression test results.

Dependent Variable: Log(CO2)			
Sample: 1990–2014			
Included observations: 11			
Variable	Coefficient	t-Statistic	Std. Error
Constant	−9.16 *	−3.62	2.53
log(GDP)	2.27 *	3.99	0.57
$\log^2$(GDP)	−0.12 *	−3.49	0.04
log(FDI)	−0.03	−1.56	0.02
log(Energy)	0.71 *	4.19	0.17
log(Trade)	−0.16 **	−1.91	0.08
R-squared		0.96	
Adjusted R-squared		0.95	
Sum of squared residuals (SSR)		1.13	
Residual sum of squares (RSS)		0.05	
F-statistic		92.94	
Prob(F-statistic)		0.00	

Source: Authors' calculations. Note: * 1% significance level; ** 10% significance level.

The next step is to check the adequacy and reliability of the obtained data.

Durbin–Watson (DW) statistic is a test of possible presence of serial correlation of residuals. Values of the DW criterion range on the interval DW_1-DW_2, where DW_1 is the lower limit, DW_2 is the upper limit. The actual values of the criterion are compared with critical values for the number of observations n and the number of independent variables m at the selected confidence level a.

If the $DW_{fact} < DW_1$, the residuals have autocorrelation. If $DW_{fact} > DW_2$, the hypothesis about the absence of auto-correlation is accepted. If $DW_1 < DW_{fact} < DW_2$ concrete conclusions cannot be obtained. In this model, $DW_{fact} = 1.10$ and $DW_1 = 0.95$, $DW_2 = 1.89$, which cannot determine the existence or absence of the autocorrelation in the sample (0.95 < 1.10 < 1.89).

The next step is to check the model for stationarity using the expanded Dickey–Fuller test, which assumes that the null hypothesis confirms non stationarity of the applied data. If t-statistics > Augmented Dickey–Fuller (ADF) critical value, then the hypothesis that data is non stationary is rejected; if t-statistics < ADF critical value, the null hypothesis is accepted or, in other words, unit root exists.

The obtained results show that the test statistic for the CO2 time series is substantially lower than all of the critical values −3.74 ($t_{1\%}$), −2.99 ($t_{5\%}$), −2.64 ($t_{10\%}$) > −4.99 (ADF). Thus, the hypothesis that investigated time series is non stationary is rejected (Figure 4). The same conclusion was made for other indicators of the regression model.

Null Hypothesis: LN_CO2_ has a unit root
Exogenous: Constant
Lag Length: 0 (Automatic - based on SIC, maxlag=5)

		t-Statistic	Prob.*
Augmented Dickey-Fuller test statistic		−4.992292	0.0005
Test critical values:	1% level	−3.737853	
	5% level	−2.991878	
	10% level	−2.635542	

*MacKinnon (1996) one-sided p-values.

Figure 4. Results of the check on the stationary time series in the EViews program.

According to the regression analysis the estimated regression line can be presented as the following:

$$logCO2 = -9.16 + 2.27GDP - 0.12GDP^2 - 0.03FDI + 0.71Energy - 0.15Trade \qquad (2)$$

This implies that for each percent increase in Energy, CO2 emission increases with 0.7 percent, and for each percentage increase in FDI and Trade, CO2 emission decreases with 0.03 and 0.15 units respectively.

The results also indicate significant positive relationship between GDP and CO2. The estimated results showed that a one percent increase in GDP leads to increase of CO2 by 2.27 percent. This change is statistically significant at a p-value (two-tail) of 0.001 with t-statistics = 3.99.

If we look to the energy consumption impact on CO2 emissions, we find a significant increase (coefficient is 0.71 and p-value = 0.136). In addition, t-statistics show how far the estimated coefficient is from zero, which is calculated in terms of standard deviations. It should be noted that the variable Energy has the highest level of t-statistic—4.19.

Empirical findings indicate that FDI has a positive effect on CO2. This means that one percent increase in FDI leads to decrease of emission level by 0.03 percent. This relationship is significant (p-value = 0.0005) and at the same time a standard error of the estimated coefficient is the lowest (Std. Error = 0.02).

A similar situation is observed with Trade: one percent increase in trade openness decreases CO2 levels by 0.16 percent. The relationship is significant with a p-value = 0.071. These analyses prove the statement that in emerging economies FDI and trade openness have positive influence on environment and lead to economic growth at the same time.

According to the regression results, the coefficient of the logarithm of GDP is positive (2.27) and the coefficient of the logarithm of squared GDP is negative (−0.12). Hence, there is an inverted U-shaped relationship between economic growth and CO2 emission. Thus, in this case, the environmental Kuznets curve hypothesis can be accepted.

Therefore, this study preliminarily validates the EKC hypothesis in Eastern European countries: the turning point is 9.18. Figure 5 shows that after the inflection point, CO2 emissions tend to decline with economic growth. It should be mentioned that not every country reached that point.

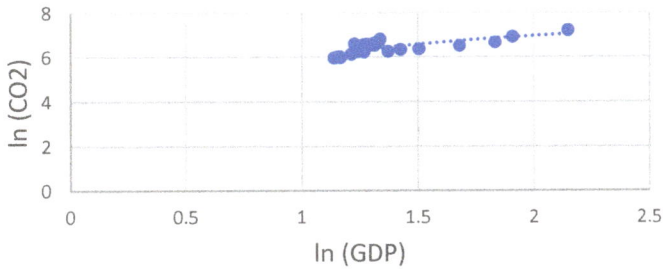

Figure 5. Environmental Kuznets curve (EKC) for carbon emissions and economic growth in Eastern European countries. Source: Authors' calculations.

A similar Kuznets curve is also estimated for eleven developed countries, with very high human development according to the HDI, the results show that after the inflection point is reached, carbon emissions begin to decrease with further economic growth, as shown in Figure 6. Moreover, this point was reached in 2003. In consequence, these results support the EKC hypothesis.

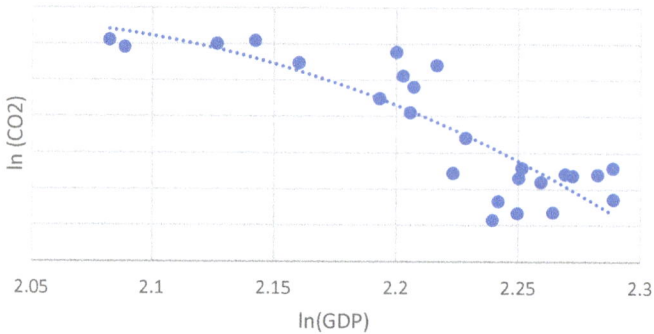

Figure 6. EKC for carbon emission and economic growth in developed countries. Source: Authors' calculations.

According to the regression analysis the regression line for developed countries can be presented as follows:

$$logCO2 = -33.43 + 6.64 GDP - 0.32 GDP^2 - 0.01 FDI + 0.45 Energy + 0.01 Trade \qquad (3)$$

To conclude, the influence of FDI for emerging and for developed economies on CO2 emission is negative. Hence, it decreases the environmental degradation level. Energy consumption has a positive impact on environmental pollution for both groups, but in Eastern European and Central Asian countries this level is stronger. In contrast, trade openness decreases the environmental degradation level in emerging economies, while in developed countries it shows another tendency (for each unit increase in Trade, CO2 emission increases with 0.01 units). In other words, developed countries produce more goods, so they need more permissions to do that. That proves, according to the Kyoto agreement, countries that produce less CO2, can sell surplus quotas to other countries that are exceeding their limits and acquiring the right to increase emissions.

4.2. Income Elasticity of Environmental Degradation

The analytical assessment of income elasticity coefficients allows one to identify the degree of influence of environmental degradation on economic growth. Hence, it is necessary to calculate the relative change in average CO2 emissions per capita for every percent change in GDP per capita in each Eastern European and Central Asian country. Income elasticity of environmental degradation can be presented as follows:

$$E_{GDP_t}^{CO2_t} = \frac{\partial CO2_t}{\partial GDP_t} * \left[\left(\sum_{t=1}^{N} \frac{GDP_t}{CO2_t}\right)/N\right] \qquad (4)$$

Table 2 describes the income elasticity of CO2 emissions for Eastern Europe and Central Asia. The computed CO2 emissions varies between 0.48 and 11.95 metric tons per capita, and real GDP per capita ranges between 438.16 to 4851.06 US$ annual for every country in the 25-year period 1990-2014.

Table 2 shows that among eleven countries, Armenia is the least elastic country within this analysis, with a coefficient of 0.091 at this level. The results show that Kazakhstan and Ukraine have the most sensitive change in economic development in respect to its CO2 changes—0.690 and 0.604 respectively. The income elasticities also indicate that CO2 emission for the individual emerging economies has different impact on economic development. Also, it should be noticed that only Tajikistan has negative elasticity, meaning that in this country the relationship between its real GDP per capita and environmental degradation is inelastic (should be added, Tajikistan has the lowest level of income per capita and the lowest level of CO2 emissions).

Table 2. Income elasticity of CO2 emissions for individual countries in Eastern Europe and Central Asia.

Country	Average CO2 (Metric tons per Capita)	Average Real GDP per Capita (Current US$)	Income Elasticity of CO2
Armenia	1.37	1659.24	0.091
Azerbaijan	4.18	2455.27	0.441
Bulgaria	6.33	3692.71	0.517
Belarus	6.28	3324.98	0.527
Georgia	1.48	1754.22	0.102
Kazakhstan	11.95	4589.37	0.690
Kyrgyz Republic	1.31	612.18	0.085
Moldova	1.89	1055.71	0.170
Romania	4.75	4403.65	0.422
Tajikistan	0.48	438.16	−0.323
Ukraine	7.21	1875.36	0.604

Source: Authors' calculations.

To sum up, empirical investigation of EKC shows us a strong influence of energy consumption on CO2 emissions.

Energy seems to be the main intensive factor of growth and development of both as industrial, as innovative modern economy (The Global Commission on the Economy and Climate 2018).

The total amount of electricity generated worldwide increased almost three times during last 30-year period), from 9882.22 TWh in 1985, 14,916.79 TWh in 1999, and finally 25,551.28 TWh in 2017.

At the beginning North America was the leader and generated 33% of the world electricity. According to BP Statistical Review of World Energy (2018), some Eastern European countries belonging to the Commonwealth of Independent States (CIS) group, and it took the 4th position at the beginning of the investigated period. The situation rapidly changed during the last 30 years and Asia Pacific became the main active producer of energy with a share of 45%. If we talk about CIS countries, the electricity generation decreased by 11%.

Figure 7 depicts the share of electricity generation by fuels by region in 2017.

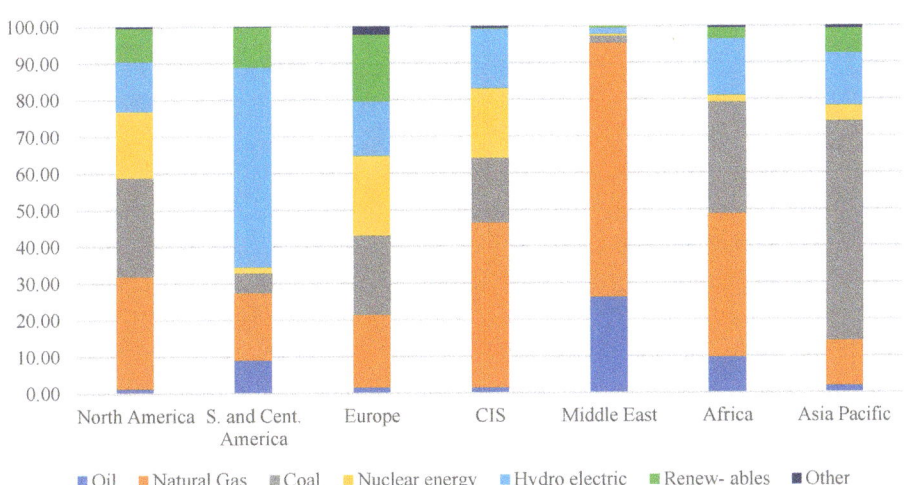

Figure 7. Regional electricity generation by fuels, 2017. CIS: Commonwealth of Independent States. Source: BP Statistical Review of World Energy (2018).

It should be noticed that the share of renewables is extremely low in the CIS countries, meanwhile the share of natural gas and coal is very high. If we compare with data of Europe in general, there is a better tendency (percentages of electricity generation by fuels have almost equal shares of total generation). This implies a good diversification in electricity generation in these countries.

Concerning regional energy consumption, there is a steady growth in several developing countries, especially in Asia (+4%). China became the world's largest energy consumer (23% of the total). Another tendency is presented in North America—where consumption has generally declined by 5%. The same tendency can be observed in countries of CIS group, when Europe has a stronger decline of 8%.

It should be noted that throughout the period of independence of the Eastern European and Central Asian countries, the energy sector remains the most vulnerable segment of the economy. Main problems seem to be: energy intensity of GDP, carbon intensity of GDP, and high level of CO_2 emission. For example, in this context, the Energy Strategy of Ukraine until 2030[1], approved by the Cabinet of Ministers, set fixed key targets. Presently the document was changed and a new Action Plan for implementation of the Energy Strategy of Ukraine until 2035[2] "Safety, Energy Efficiency, and Competitiveness" (2018) was approved. Nevertheless, none of the strategic goals were achieved (reducing the energy intensity of GDP, intensifying the development of own energy resources, diversifying sources and routes of energy supplies, creating a strategic oil reserve, creating elements of the nuclear fuel cycle, and comprehensive development of alternative energy).

4.3. Energy Intensity of GDP

The analysis reveals that the energy intensity level of Eastern European and Central Asian countries exceeds most limits, e.g., in Ukraine it is the highest among the group, furthermore, the intensity level two times higher than the average world level and almost three times higher than in the EU (Table 3).

Table 3. Energy intensity level of primary energy, MJ/$2011 PPP GDP.

Country	1990	2010	2011	2012	2013	2014	2015
Armenia	24.37	5.39	5.63	5.75	5.43	5.35	5.38
Azerbaijan	15.57	3.36	3.64	3.88	3.72	3.76	3.73
Bulgaria	14.60	6.63	7.02	6.69	6.09	6.36	6.38
Belarus	23.13	7.73	7.81	7.98	7.06	6.83	6.47
Kazakhstan	13.83	8.47	8.84	8.07	8.42	7.87	7.92
Kyrgyz Republic	20.54	7.58	8.61	10.76	9.26	9.21	8.64
Moldova	17.40	10.50	9.71	9.68	7.95	8.16	8.39
Romania	10.05	4.17	4.22	4.09	3.61	3.48	3.52
Russian Federation	12.03	8.73	8.78	8.70	8.46	8.35	8.41
Tajikistan	11.54	5.66	5.29	5.29	5.46	5.06	5.01
Ukraine	19.38	15.41	14.00	13.52	12.82	12.49	11.79
European Union	5.63	4.21	3.98	3.96	3.91	3.70	3.66

Source: The World Bank (2019).

This is mainly due to the high degree of wear of domestic infrastructure, in particular energy infrastructure, low efficiency of use of fuel and energy resources in technological processes. It should be noted, the use of electric power in these emerging economies can be divided by types of power plants, which produce electricity, i.e., hydro, atomic, thermal power and other renewable. For example, the biggest share of energy in Ukraine is produced precisely at thermal power plants. A problem with these plants is that they remain the largest pollutants of the atmosphere.

Also it should be noted that the level of energy intensity in these countries decreased since their independence year, but despite of this fact is still remains extremely high.

---

[1] Energy Strategy of Ukraine until 2030. Approved by the Cabinet of Ministers No.1071 on July 24, 2013.
[2] The Energy Strategy of Ukraine until 2035 "Safety, Energy Efficiency and Competitiveness". Approved by the Cabinet of Ministers No.1071 on June 6, 2018.

4.4. Carbon Intensity of GDP

The CO2 intensity shows a similar tendency. The intensity of carbon emissions from fossil fuel combustion in Eastern European and Central Asian countries has decreased almost by 50% during the period from 1990 to 2016. At the same time, the carbon intensity still remains the highest (e.g., in Ukraine this level exceeds the CO2 intensity of Poland by 1.8, Germany—by 2.8, and is 2 times higher than the world level) (Table 4).

Table 4. CO2 emission intensity at constant parity of purchasing power, kg CO2/$ 2005.

Country	1990	2000	2010	2011	2012	2013	2014	2015	2016
Ukraine	1.34	1.37	0.86	0.85	0.83	0.80	0.73	0.65	0.67
Poland	1.17	0.65	0.48	0.45	0.43	0.43	0.39	0.37	0.36
Germany	0.44	0.32	0.27	0.25	0.25	0.26	0.24	0.24	0.24
World	0.50	0.42	0.38	0.37	0.36	0.36	0.35	0.34	0.32

Source: World Energy Statistics (2018). Yearbook. Note: CO2 intensity is the ratio of CO2 emissions from fuel combustion and gross domestic product (GDP) and measures the amount of CO2 emissions to create one unit of GDP. CO2 emissions cover only emissions from the combustion of fossil fuels (coal, oil, and gas).

4.5. Level of CO2 Emissions

It should be mentioned that presently there is a high disproportion between regional emissions and population size, e.g., North America is a home to 5% of the world population and at the same time this region emits approximately 18% of CO2. As for Africa, it has 16% of the world population, but emits only 4% of total world carbon dioxide. In fact, Asia has 60% of the world population, but the pollution level is 49% (Figure 8).

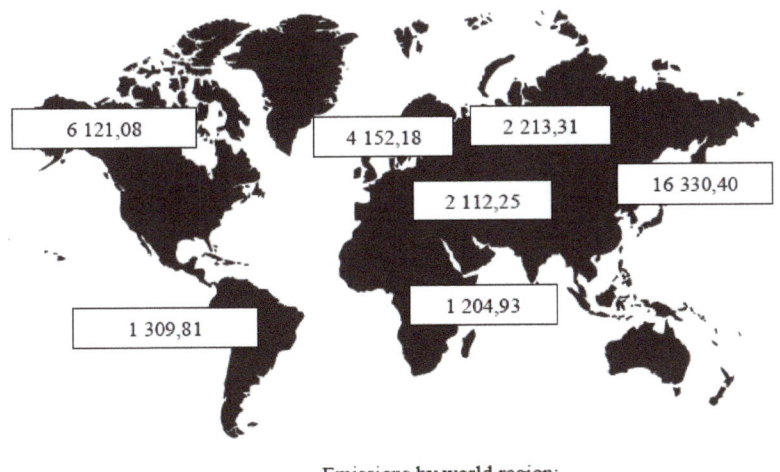

Emissions by world region:

North America – 18%
South. & Central America – 4%
Europe – 12%
CIS – 7%
Middle East – 6%
Africa – 4%
Asia Pacific – 49%

Figure 8. World carbon dioxide emissions by region (in million metric tons of carbon dioxide). Source: BP Statistical Review of World Energy (2018).

Hence, finding the compatible pathway for levelling this inequality is a great challenge.

Population growth, rising GDP levels lead to resource scarcity. Also, the regression analyses proved this statement: according to the obtained results, one percent increase in GDP leads to increase of CO2 by 2.27 percent.

Referred to the vision of Industry 4.0, it is still based on automation technology, which requires consumption of electricity, but at the same time these technologies contribute to reduction of the larger impact of many industries through the smart traffic management. Hence, this raises a valid question: how does the new technologies use affect the environmental sustainability?

4.6. Investigation of the Relationship between ICT Use and Energy Consumption

The role of Industry 4.0 is significant, however, the technologies need more and more energy, particular the ICT sector. Moreover, the obtained results proved a negative influence of energy consumption on CO_2 in emerging economies (for each percentage increase in energy, emission increases with 0.7 percent). Thus, there is a problem of energy efficiency policy in emerging economies.

In order to investigate the relationship between the ICT use and energy consumption for each region, the paper offers a correlation matrix to visualize correlation coefficients between relevant variables (Table 5).

Table 5. Correlation matrix.

Region	Correlation Coefficients, Energy vs. ICT Indicators		
	ICT1	ICT2	ICT3
Total Africa	−0.86	0.97	0.99
Total Middle East	−0.79	0.92	0.99
Total Asia Pacific	−0.90	0.98	1.00
Total CIS	0.16	0.24	0.32
Total Europe	0.67	−0.67	−0.81
Total Americas	−0.77	0.61	0.73

Source: International Telecommunication Union (2017). BP Statistical Review of World Energy (2018).

The analyses show that in CIS countries there is a positive correlation between energy consumption and ICT indicators, at the same time, the values of the coefficients are very low: ICT1 (0.16), ICT2 (0.24) and ICT3 (0.32). In Europe there is another situation—a negative relationship between two ICT indicators and energy: ICT2 (−0.67) and ICT3 (−0.81), that can be a result of active implementation of energy saving technologies in European countries. In general, the analysis shows, that the ICT sector increases the energy consumption in CIS countries.

5. Discussion

5.1. Limitations and Recommendations

This study has several limitations. First, on a sector level the study looks at indicators of the ICT sector only, which plays a key supporting role for intelligent manufacturing.

Second, this present study of the relationship between environmental degradation and economic development samples the data for eleven Eastern European and Central Asian economies for the period 1990 to 2014. Hence, it remains uncertain, if these countries have reached the turning point for CO2 emissions during the recent years.

Thus, in order to obtain more comprehensive results future research should be expanded using additional indicators to measure the impact of Industry 4.0 in a more recent period.

The results show that emerging economies have similar problems. Hence, to create a well-balanced system and improve an energy situation in terms of technological leadership of each emerging country the following pillars can be of interest:

- energy saving and energy efficiency (attraction of FDI to unleash innovation potential of the industry);
- strategic reserves (harnessing the power of the energy sector, including renewables);
- import diversification (advanced supply chain transparency);
- integration into the EU energy area (connected and synchronized energy networks).

Such a system will become one of the safe guards of the country's survival under adverse external circumstances, preserving its sovereignty, territorial integrity and further economic development.

5.2. Implications

International experience shows that social progress largely depends on maintaining a balance between the goals of supporting economic growth, business competitiveness, environmental security and reducing social inequality. In order to achieve long-term goals, certain short- and medium-term tasks must be consistently implemented along with sufficient policy measures.

Overall, it is clear that innovations play a central role in the policymaking process. Park et al. (2010) stated that technological development in the ICT sector, services, industry, agriculture and market-based policies are main strategies of ecological modernization in China. Also, it should be noted, circular economy (Garcia-Muiña et al. 2018), cleaner production (Gavrilescu 2004), low-carbon technologies (Karpa 2017), corporate social responsibility are key components of ecological modernization.

Furthermore, it is recommended for Eastern European and Central Asian economies to consider the experience of the policy implications of other developing countries, which are also struggling with striking a balance between economic growth and environmental protection (Nguyen et al. 2019). For example, Vuong (2018) highlights the significance of high-tech industries in Vietnam, which presently takes high position in the global value chain among emerging markets. At the same time, the society has been enthusiastic for technology and startups in recent years. But in fact, this situation leads to some changes in Vietnamese agriculture, finance, and banking, and even Hanoi urban (Vuong 2019).

Bocken et al. (2014) have pointed out that for successful adoption of sustainable business models it is needed to combine innovations, technology, new innovative approaches to collaboration and education, and to raise awareness to facilitate and obtain application of the system perspective.

Also, this approach is widespread nowadays, some researchers have already offered actionable recommendations on how to mitigate and curb the explosive industry sector global greenhouse gas emissions footprint, through a combination of renewable energy use, tax policies, managerial actions, and alternative business models (Belkhir and Elmeligi 2018).

Moreover, the results show that some Eastern European countries, which are members of EU, nowadays implements different tools toward the protection of environment and provides effective energy saving policy. Thus, the situation in these economies has improved substantially. Also, the institutional development index of these countries shows huge differences between the EU members and other Eastern European and Central Asian countries, e.g., Bulgaria and Romania at the top and Tajikistan at the bottom of the list (Grytten and Koilo 2019).

To sum up, the obtained results prove that implementation of new technologies have huge impact on energy consumption, which presently leads to environmental degradation in some regions.

6. Conclusions

The present study empirically investigates the long-run relationship between carbon dioxide emissions, economic growth, net FDI inflows, energy intensity, and trade openness.

According to the data analysis, the following conclusions was obtained: the results confirm the carbon emission's Kuznets curve hypothesis in Eastern Europe and Central Asia. The relationship between carbon emission and economic growth tends to follow an inverted U-shaped Kuznets curve.

Also, estimated income elasticities of CO_2 emissions for individual countries in Eastern Europe and Central Asia perform differently. The paper concludes that within a group Ukraine and Kazakhstan has the most sensitive change in economic growth in respect to its CO_2. At the same time, Tajikistan has a negative elasticity, thus in this country the relationship between its real GDP per capita and environmental degradation is inelastic.

The results confirm that some emerging economies have already reached the point, when the environmental situation can be improved and sustainable goals can be achieved. Based on above mentioned results derived from this study the following conclusions can be obtained: politics, which are based on innovative transition to a low-carbon economy can offer great opportunities for economic growth and achieving the sustainable development goals.

Industry 4.0 could promote significant environmental, economic, and social benefits, therefore, new technologies should strive to contribute towards a more "sustainable development" and promote energy conservation in order to reduce carbon emissions.

Nevertheless, the results show that ICT sector has a different impact on sustainability in different regions, e.g., new technologies use increases the energy consumption in CIS countries, while in Europe there is another tendency. As long as energy intensity and carbon intensity levels remain high in emerging economies, there is a need for further investigation of the relationship between technology use and CO2 emissions. Moreover, future studies should be expanded using additional indicators to measure the impact of Industry 4.0 on sustainability.

Funding: This research received no external funding.

Conflicts of Interest: The authors declare no conflict of interest.

References

Annen, Kurt. 2006. HP-Filter Excel Add-In. Available online: https://web-reg.de/webreg-hodrick-prescott-filter/ (accessed on 12 May 2019).

Belkhir, Lotfi, and Ahmed Elmeligi. 2018. Assessing ICT global emissions footprint: Trends to 2040 & recommendations. *Journal of Cleaner Production* 177: 448–63.

Bertoldi, Paolo, Maria Avgerinou, and Luca Castellazzi. 2017. *Trends in Data Centre Energy Consumption under the European Code of Conduct for Data Centre Energy Efficiency*. Luxembourg: Publications Office of the European Union.

Blunck, Erskin, and Hedwig Werthmann. 2017. Industry 4.0—An Opportunity to Realize Sustainable Manufacturing and its Potential for a Circular Economy. *Microeconomics* 3: 645–66.

Bocken, Nancy M. P., Samuel W. Short, Padmakshi Rana, and Steve Evans. 2014. A literature and practice review to develop sustainable business model archetypes. *Journal of Cleaner Production* 65: 42–56. [CrossRef]

Bonilla, Silvia, Helton Silva, Marcia Terra da Silva, Rodrigo Franco Gonçalves, and José Sacomano. 2018. Industry 4.0 and Sustainability Implications: A Scenario-Based Analysis of the Impacts and Challenges. *Sustainability* 10: 3740. [CrossRef]

BP Statistical Review of World Energy. 2018. Centre for Energy Economics Research and Policy, Heriot-Watt University (67th ed.). Available online: https://www.bp.com/content/dam/bp/business-sites/en/global/corporate/pdfs/energy-economics/statistical-review/bp-stats-review-2018-full-report.pdf (accessed on 17 May 2019).

Buzan, Barry, Ole Wæver, Ole Wæver, and Jaap De Wilde. 1998. *Security: A New Framework for Analysis*. Boulder: Lynne Rienner, p. 239.

Environmental Defense Fund. 2018. Business and the Fourth Wave of Environmentalism. Available online: https://www.edf.org/sites/default/files/documents/business_and_the_fourth_wave.pdf (accessed on 17 May 2019).

The Environmental Performance Index. 2018. Yale University. Available online: https://epi.envirocenter.yale.edu/ (accessed on 17 May 2019).

EViews. 2019. Unit Root Testing. Available online: http://www.eviews.com/help/helpintro.html#page/content/advtimeser-Unit_Root_Testing.html (accessed on 17 May 2019).

Frankel, Jeffrey A., and Andrew K. Rose. 2005. Is Trade Good or Bad for the Environment? Sorting Out the Causality. *The Review of Economics and Statistics* 87: 85–91. [CrossRef]

Garcia-Muiña, Fernando, Rocío González-Sánchez, Anna Ferrari, and Davide Settembre-Blundo. 2018. The Paradigms of Industry 4.0 and Circular Economy as Enabling Drivers for the Competitiveness of Businesses and Territories: The Case of an Italian Ceramic Tiles Manufacturing Company. *Social Sciences* 7: 255. [CrossRef]

Gavrilescu, Maria. 2004. Cleaner production as a tool for sustainable development. *Environmental Engineering and Management Journal* 3: 45–70. [CrossRef]

Grytten, Ola Honningdal, and Viktoriia Koilo. 2019. The Financial Instability Hypothesis and the Financial Crisis in Eastern European Emerging Economies. Available online: https://papers.ssrn.com/sol3/papers.cfm?abstract_id=3381533 (accessed on 11 May 2019).

Hisamatsu, Hiroyuki, and Koichi Maekawa. 1994. The distribution of the Durbin–Watson statistic in integrated and near-integrated models. *Journal of Econometrics* 61: 367–82. [CrossRef]

The Division for Sustainable Development Goals (DSDG). 2019. The High-Level Political Forum on Sustainable Development in 2019 (HLPF 2019). Available online: https://sustainabledevelopment.un.org/hlpf/2019/ (accessed on 12 May 2019).

Holden, Erling, Kristin Linnerud, David Banister, Valeria Jana Schwanitz, and August Wierling. 2017. The Imperatives of Sustainable Development. *Sustainable Development* 25: 213–26. [CrossRef]

Human Development Index. 2017. United Nations Development Programme. Available online: http://www.hdr.undp.org/en/data (accessed on 17 May 2019).

International Telecommunication Union. 2017. TU World Telecommunication. ICT Indicators Data. Available online: https://www.itu.int/en/ITU-D/Statistics/Pages/stat/default.aspx (accessed on 22 June 2019).

Kacar, S. Burak, and M. Ozgur Kayalica. 2014. Environmental Kuznets Curve and sulfur emissions: A comparative econometric analyzis. *Environmental Economics* 5: 8–20.

Kagermann, Henning, Wolf-Dieter Lukas, and Wolfgang Wahlster. 2011. Industrie 4.0: Mitdem Internet der Dinge auf dem Weg zur 4. Industriellen Revolution. *VDI Nachrichten* 13. Available online: http://www.wolfgang-wahlster.de/wordpress/wp-content/uploads/Industrie_4_0_Mit_dem_Internet_der_Dinge_auf_dem_Weg_zur_vierten_industriellen_Revolution_2.pdf (accessed on 11 May 2019).

Kagermann, Henning, Wolfgang Wahlster, and Johannes Helbig. 2013. Securing the Future of German Manufacturing Industry: Recommendations for Implementing the Strategic Initiative INDUSTRIE 4.0, Final Report of the Industrie 4.0 Working Group. Available online: https://www.din.de/blob/76902/e8cac883f42bf28536e7e8165993f1fd/recommendations-for-implementing-industry-4-0-data.pdf (accessed on 30 June 2019).

Karpa, Waldemar. 2017. The Effect of Low-Carbon Innovations on Reducing Environmental Threats to Health. *Journal of Innovation Economics & Management* 24: 89–104.

Kaya, Gizem, Merve Kumaş, and Burc Ulengin. 2017. The role of foreign direct investment and trade on carbon emissions in Turkey. *Environmental Economics* 8: 8–17. [CrossRef]

Lee, Jay, Hossein Davari, Jaskaran Singh, and Vibhor Pandhare. 2018. Industrial Artificial Intelligence for Industry 4.0-based Manufacturing Systems. *Manufacturing Letters* 18: 20–23. [CrossRef]

Manoukian, Jean-Grégoire. 2018. Industry 4.0 meets the 4th Wave of Environmentalism. Available online: https://enablon.com/blog/2018/06/28/industry-4-0-meets-the-4th-wave-of-environmentalism (accessed on 12 May 2019).

Nguyen, Viet-Ha T., Thu-Trang Vuong, Manh-Tung Ho, and Quan-Hoang Vuong. 2019. The new politics of debt in the transition economy of Vietnam Hong-Kong. *Austrian Journal of South-East Asian Studies* 12: 91–110.

Panayotou, Theodore. 1993. *Empirical Tests and Policy Analysis of Environmental Degradation at Different Stages of Economic Development*. Geneva: International Labour Organization.

Park, Jacob, Joseph Sarkis, and Zhaohui Wu. 2010. Creating integrated business and environmental value within the context of China's circular economy and ecological modernization. *Journal of Cleaner Production* 18: 1494–501. [CrossRef]

Pouri, Maria J., and Lorenz M. Hilty. 2018. Conceptualizing the Digital Sharing Economy in the Context of Sustainability. *Sustainability* 12: 4453. [CrossRef]

PricewaterhouseCoopers. 2016. Industry 4.0: Building the Digital Enterprise. 2016 Global Industry 4.0 Survey. Available online: https://www.pwc.com/id/en/CIPS/assets/industry-4.0-building-your-digital-enterprise.pdf (accessed on 12 May 2019).

Shahbaz, Muhammad, and Avik Sinha. 2018. Environmental Kuznets Curve for CO2 Emission: A Literature Survey, MPRA Paper. Available online: https://mpra.ub.uni-muenchen.de/86281/ (accessed on 17 May 2019).

Stern, David I. 2004. The rise and fall of the environmental Kuznets curve. *World Development* 32: 1419–39. [CrossRef]

The Global Commission on the Economy and Climate. 2018. Unlocking the Inclusive Growth Story of the 21st Century: Accelerating Climate Action in Urgent Times. Available online: https://newclimateeconomy.report/2018/wp-content/uploads/sites/6/2018/09/NCE_2018_FULL-REPORT.pdf (accessed on 19 May 2019).

The World Bank. 2019. *World Development Indicators*. Washington, DC: World Bank, Available online: https://data.worldbank.org/indicator (accessed on 17 May 2019).

Tjoek, Patrick Wijaya, and PI Wu. 2018. Exploring the environmental Kuznets curve for CO2 and SO2 for Southeast Asia in the 21st century context. *Environmental Economics* 9: 7–21. [CrossRef]

Vuong, Quan-Hoang. 2018. The (ir)rational consideration of the cost of science in transition economies. *Nature Human Behaviour* 2: 5. [CrossRef]

Vuong, Quan-Hoang. 2019. Computational Entrepreneurship: From Economic Complexities to Interdisciplinary Research. *Problems and Perspectives in Management* 17: 117–29. [CrossRef]

Vuong, Quan-Hoang, Manh-Tung Ho, and NGUYỄN Minh Hoàng. 2019. Exploring OECD SDGs Pilot City's 50-Year Time Series Data and Its Environmental Kuznets Curves. Working Paper No. PKU-1907. Available online: https://doi.org/10.31219/osf.io/aexcd (accessed on 4 July 2019).

World Energy Statistics. 2018. Yearbook. Energy Consulting Services on the World Energy Market—Enerdata. Available online: https://yearbook.enerdata.ru/co2-fuel-combustion/world-CO2-intensity.html (accessed on 17 May 2019).

WWF. 2017. Sustainability, Stability, Security. Available online: http://d2ouvy59p0dg6k.cloudfront.net/downloads/embargoed_14nov_rapport3s_en_27102017.pdf (accessed on 18 May 2019).

Xu, Hengzhou, Chuanrong Zhang, Weidong Li, Wenjing Zhang, and Hongchun Yin. 2018. Economic growth and carbon emission in China. *Proceedings of Rijeka Faculty of Economics* 36: 11–28.

Zaied, Younes Ben, Nidhaleddine Ben Cheikh, and Pascal Nguyen. 2017. Longrun analysis of Environmental Kuznets Curve in the Middle East and North Africa. *Environmental Economics* 8: 72–79. [CrossRef]

© 2019 by the author. Licensee MDPI, Basel, Switzerland. This article is an open access article distributed under the terms and conditions of the Creative Commons Attribution (CC BY) license (http://creativecommons.org/licenses/by/4.0/).

Article

When the Poor Buy the Rich: New Evidence on Wealth Effects of Cross-Border Acquisitions

Hong-Hai Ho [1], Thi-Hanh Vu [2], Ngoc-Tien Dao [3], Manh-Tung Ho [4,5,*] and Quan-Hoang Vuong [4,5,6,*]

[1] Faculty of Finance and Banking, Foreign Trade University, 91 Chua Lang Street, Hanoi 100000, Vietnam; hai.ho@ftu.edu.vn
[2] Institute of Economics and International Business, Foreign Trade University, 91 Chua Lang Street, Hanoi 100000, Vietnam; hanhvt@ftu.edu.vn
[3] Institute of Economics and International Trade, Foreign Trade University, 91 Chua Lang Street, Hanoi 100000, Vietnam; dntien@ftu.edu.vn
[4] Center for Interdisciplinary Social Research, Phenikaa University, Yen Nghia, Ha Dong District, Hanoi 100803, Vietnam
[5] Faculty of Economics and Finance, Phenikaa University, Yen Nghia, Ha Dong District, Hanoi 100803, Vietnam
[6] Centre Emile Bernheim, Université Libre de Bruxelles, 50 Ave. F.D. Roosevelt, 1050 Brussels, Belgium
* Correspondence: tung.homanh@phenikaa-uni.edu.vn (M.-T.H.); hoang.vuongquan@phenikaa-uni.edu.vn or qvuong@ulb.ac.be (Q.-H.V.)

Received: 30 May 2019; Accepted: 18 June 2019; Published: 19 June 2019

Abstract: The growing trend of merging and acquisition (M&A) investments from emerging to developed market economies over the last two decades motivates the question on the long-run effects of M&A on the wealth of emerging markets. This paper contributes to the current literature on cross-border M&A (CBMA) by focusing on the long-term effects of this event on the bidder's stock return in emerging markets. To address the challenges of finding an accurate measure for the effects, this study applies the propensity score matching framework in tandem with difference-in-differences (DID) on a comprehensive dataset over the 1990–2010 period. The analyses show evidence of systematic detrimental impacts of cross-border M&A on shareholders' welfare in the long run, to a certain extent, diverging from the existing literature, which mainly highlights the positive effects for certain types of M&A. The striking finding is that such strong negative effects remain persistent even when various factors previously known as capable of suppressing underperformance are considered. Our study is in line with the growing landscape of cross-border mergers and acquisitions from the "poor" to the "rich" countries.

Keywords: M&A; wealth effects; propensity score matching; emerging markets

1. Introduction

With the arrival of Industry 4.0 and the shifting landscape of entrepreneurial finance in recent years, cross-border mergers and acquisitions (CBMA) have recorded growth in both values, as well as in the number of deals across different regions in recent years (OECD 2017). More impressive in this development is the embedded growth of international acquisitions from emerging to developed countries. By 2013, the number of deals made by emerging-market companies had accounted for 37% of the world market for cross-border deals, having recorded annual double-digit growth from 2000 to 2013 (Cogman et al. 2015). In terms of value, the figure skyrocketed by 929% from US$17 billion in 2003 to US$175 billion in 2013 (UNCTAD 2014). The remarkable increase of M&A from emerging countries is often driven by the advanced technology, brand names, and natural resources of target firms

(Cogman et al. 2015; Deng 2013; Deng and Yang 2015; Lebedev et al. 2015). While much of the M&A literature has shed light on various aspects of CBMA (e.g., the motivation, the strategic implication, and the market reaction), it is surprising that little is known about the wealth effects of M&A events on the acquiring firms in emerging markets. Given that firms from emerging and developed markets face asymmetries in corporate governance, institutional environments, and financial practices (Boateng and Huang 2017; Chari et al. 2009; Young et al. 2008), extending the literature on the wealth effects of acquirers from less-developed markets could consolidate the current cross-border M&A trend, especially in the wake of computational entrepreneurship (Vuong 2019).

This paper aims to bridge the gap in the literature concerning the long-term effects of CBMA events on the bidder's stock return in emerging markets. One of the challenges in the long-run study is the accuracy of the measure (Sudarsanam and Mahate 2003). The incremental return as a result of the CBMA event is traditionally measured as the difference between observed return and the estimated return using a market (i.e., single index) model. While such a method is acceptable in the short-run study, as the firm risk is relatively stable, it is fundamentally flawed for long-run investigation, because the genuine effect of the CBMA event cannot be isolated from the organic growth of the firm in the course of months or years, resulting in bias estimates (Jensen and Ruback 1983). Alternatively, Barber and Lyon (1997), Spiess and Affleck-Graves (1995), and Loughran and Ritter (1995) used a matching method that benchmarks the observed return against the return of the *matched firm* (firm having similar size and market-to-book). Essentially, this method trades off the assumption that the firm risk stays unchanged after the M&A event (i.e., market model) with the assumption that firms with similar ex-ante characteristics yield the same ex-post return. It is possible to improve the accuracy of the latter method by matching firms upon several characteristics with a propensity score matching (PSM) model. Even though PSM allows for multi-dimensional matching, it is still vulnerable to temporal time-invariant and unobservable selection bias. Such bias, however, could be fixed when combing PSM with a difference-in-differences (DIDs) estimation technique (Blundell and Dias 2000; Girma et al. 2003). As a result, this paper employs DIDs in tandem with PSM to answer the following research questions:

RQ1: What are the long-term wealth effects of CBMAs on shareholders' return in emerging markets?

RQ2: How would the wealth effects change when controlling for factors such as related industry, payment method, acquisition for control, prior experience, and structure break, which are known to have positive impacts on the outcome of M&As?

The current study is structured as follows: Section 2 explores the agency problem and reviews the literature on CBMA wealth effects and their determinants. Section 3 explains the data and methodology, while Section 4 discusses the findings and their implications. The paper ends with the concluding remarks in Section 5.

2. Literature Review

2.1. The Wealth Effects of CBMA of an Emerging-Market Acquirer

Within the extant finance literature, findings remain inconclusive over whether such acquisition enhances or decreases the value of the acquiring firm. Martynova and Renneboog (2009) conducted a meta-analysis on M&A and documented series of significant evidence that the value of bidding firms tends to decline over several years after the M&A. However, the evidence of negative long-run abnormal return disappears when certain types of acquisitions are taken into consideration. For instance, Sudarsanam and Mahate (2003) and Mitchell and Stafford (2000) find cash-financed outperforms stock-financed for acquirers with a high market-to-book ratio (Glamour firm). Franks and Harris (1989) show that hostile bids generate better value to acquirers than friendly bids in a three-year event window; consistently, Cosh and Guest (2001) find significant long-run abnormal returns for hostile takeovers. In addition, Bradley and Sundaram (2004) report evidence showing that the acquiring of a listed target yields a higher return than taking over a private target in the long run. Recently, Bhabra and Huang (2013) found strong evidence of improved shareholder value over three years following the M&A, especially for transactions involving state-owned enterprise, payment in cash, domestic target, and related industry. The mixture of evidence suggests that the wealth effect is contingent on the characteristics of the acquirers, the transactions specifics, and the environment settings. Such conditions vary among groups of acquirers. Therefore, it is unlikely to generalize the findings in developed countries in the emerging counterparts, despite the abundance of studies found in the former nations.

2.2. The Characteristics of M&A from Emerging to Developed Markets

The agency problem arises from moral hazard and information asymmetry, and it is often cited as one of the major drivers of all strategic managerial decisions, including M&A (Jensen and Meckling 1976). In emerging countries, the managerial entrenchment could be more severe because of their particular ownership structure. In China, for example, large bidders are often controlled by the Government, who has the right to assign a chief executive officer (CEO). However, CEOs in the state-owned enterprises are normally rooted from political connection, hence enjoying protection in exchange for offering lucrative opportunities to government agencies (Faccio 2010; Luo 2001; Sheng et al. 2011; Sun et al. 2012). Such a bureaucratic mechanism inflicts damage to creditors and public shareholders (Radelet et al. 1998).

Additionally, Gibson (2003) argues that stock ownership in emerging countries is not well diffused, because a large portion of emerging-market firms is small- and medium-sized, often controlled by founding families (Bhaumik and Gregoriou 2010; Bhaumik and Driffield 2011). A typical family firm often operates on a unique design, which has proven successful in the domestic market for generations. CBMA to more advanced markets dominated by large enterprises might lead to a change in such a business model and potential corporate cultural conflict in the integration phase (Gallo and Sveen 1991). These factors are frequently referred to as detrimental to shareholders' wealth. Thus, given the distinctive state ownership and dominant family holding, the wealth effect might be different between emerging and developed markets.

Dunning et al. (2007) argued that international expansion via M&A requires certain proprietary advantages to create synergies such as ownership, location, and internalization (i.e., eclectic paradigm). While developed-market acquirers normally have access to privileged technology, high-end markets, and superior management skills, an emerging-market counterpart owns a different set of advantages, namely the ability to gather a huge low-cost labor force on short notice or the capability of dealing with political instability (Guillén and García-Canal 2009). Such advantages entail not only different synergies, but also different motivation for emerging-market acquirers. For example, the acquisition of intangible assets such as patents, trademarks, brand name, and distribution network in the developed nation is regularly found in various studies on emerging countries (Antkiewicz and Whalley 2006; Deng 2004; Grimpe and Hussinger 2009; Guillén and García-Canal 2009). The differences in synergy and motivation should reflect in the ex post performance of the CBMA transaction.

2.3. Determinants of CBMA Wealth Effects in Emerging Markets

2.3.1. Industry Relatedness

Industrial relatedness has been widely debated in finance and strategic management literature. Several studies argue that acquiring related target (firms having the same Standard Industrial Classifications (SIC) code to acquirer's) could create both operational synergies by removing duplicates, laying off workers, and enhancing absorptive capacity. Lien and Klein (2008) argue that related acquisition should create higher value to shareholders than unrelated (i.e., conglomerate or diversifying) acquisitions. By contrast, diversification may entail a low cost of borrowing or the flexibility of the internal financial market. Gatzer et al. (2014) conducted a survey of CEOs about the motive of firm diversification and found that a lower level of earnings volatility and financial distress are the most important drivers of CEO diversification decision.

Besides, the business model of a diversified firm, organized as a set of interlinked operational units financially controlled by a hub, embeds an internal capital market. Allocation of the fund through such a convenient tunnel reduces financing frictions, enhancing the financial capability, and allowing for a higher level of investment (Stein 2003). However, the privilege of the internal capital market may encourage managers' rent-seeking behavior (Scharfstein and Stein 2000), leading to either overinvestment (Matsusaka and Nanda 2002; Stulz 1990) or sub-optimal allocation of the resources (Lien and Klein 2008).

The existing empirical evidence on the performance of related mergers and acquisitions seems to be mixed. Comment and Jarrell (1995) and Bhagat et al. (1990) provide evidence of optimistic market reaction to the announcement of a firm's plan to refocus, while Servaes (1996) and Lang and Stulz (1994) find that diversified firms are traded at a discount. On the contrary, some studies find evidence rejecting the undervaluation in conglomerate acquisitions. Campa and Kedia (2002) and Graham et al. (2002) find that the causal relationship between diversification and undervaluation is spurred by common factors. Once they are controlled, the discount disappears. Similar evidence is found in Chevalier (2004) and Villalonga (2004).

In an emerging market, Khanna and Palepu (2000) report a prevalence of conglomerate acquisitions, which either favor the internal capital market privilege or indicate that emerging-market acquirers possess limited choice and yet manage to generate incremental value. Kale (2004) argued that the latter case is possible as the markets for corporate control in emerging countries are still in the infant stage, and the pioneer acquirers can still grasp the "low hanging fruits". Nonetheless, such opportunities should soon deplete, given the recent "tsunami" of outward investments from emerging nations.

2.3.2. Method of Payment

Paying for the target with cash or with stock or anything in between is not a concern if the market is theoretically efficient, as all existing information fully reflected in current stock price would eliminate the abnormal return of any news announcement. In effect, the empirical evidence documents the positive impacts of cash financing and underperformance of a stock exchange transaction (Loughran and Vijh 1997; Mitchell and Stafford 2000; Rau and Vermaelen 1998). The underlying signaling theory assumes market inefficiency, and hence each party to the M&A transaction generally seizes private information unavailable to the counterparty and the public. In such an asymmetric environment, the cash-financed acquisition announcement signals the acquirer's share being undervalued, while the stock-financing announcement signals overvaluation (Myers and Majluf 1984). The subsequent market adjustment toward the payment method in the announcement underpins a substantial movement in the market, causing significant abnormal return, not only in the short run, but also several years after the acquisition (Loughran and Vijh 1997).

Also, the classic market microstructure literature establishes that stock price and liquidity are influenced by information asymmetry (O'Hara 2003). In larger and more efficient markets, traders encounter a lower trading cost, and informed traders might extract extra return at the expense of the uninformed trader (Agudelo et al. 2015). Accordingly, acquirers in a weaker institutional setting like that in an emerging country should possess more private information, which helps them extract even more benefit from the less informed targets. Thus, we expect a stronger positive wealth effect in a cash-financing transaction in emerging than in developed countries.

2.3.3. Power of Control

The controlling ownership of target is crucial in cross-border acquisitions, as the target's management would otherwise take advantage of the incomplete contract and refrain from sharing strategic resources such as technology or management expertise. Control rights also entitle acquirers exclusive benefits of which minority shareholders are unaware. Grossman and Hart (1986) postulate that acquirers are likely to be undermined by the target's "opportunistic and distortionary" behavior unless the residual control right is attained. The empirical evidence, indeed, supports this argument, as Chari et al. (2009) find that control is the key element of positive abnormal return. If the control is not accounted for, the evidence immediately shows detrimental wealth effects. Dyck and Zingales (2004) even attempted to measure the corporate control premium, reporting that such a premium ranges from −4% (in Japan) to +65% (in Brazil). Such evidence demonstrates that the value of the control is higher in less developed countries. Thus, this paper expects positive effects of control ownership in the long run.

2.3.4. Prior Experience

An acquirer having prior experience in corporate control in developed markets can reduce the transaction and post-integration costs in subsequent attempts. Barkema et al. (1996) argue that knowledge of the foreign country such as institutional characteristics could reduce the cultural barrier on both corporate and national levels. Effectively, Aggarwal and Samwick (2003) find lessons that learned in previous encounters increase the chance of success for serial acquirers. However, it is not necessarily beneficial when the acquirers have a good track record on acquisition performance. Roll (1986) theorizes that historical successes invoke managerial hubris, which clouds the manger's judgments in subsequent transactions and hence value destruction post-acquisition. Tanna and Yousef (2019) find supporting evidence for the hubris hypothesis that experienced acquirers entail higher systematic risk. Consistently, Al Rahahleh and Wei (2012) find that firms undertaking frequent M&A also suffer from declining return. The inconsistent evidence suggests a rather unpredictable behavior of prior acquisition experience in the emerging market.

2.3.5. Structural Break

Mergers and acquisitions appear to occur in waves, each of which is characterized by a different set of conditions (Martynova and Renneboog 2009). Thus, it is necessary to consider M&A activity at different homogeneous periods (Jarrell and Bradley 1980). Empirically, Asquith et al. (1983) break their merger sample based on two periods and statistically verify the difference in wealth effects with pairwise t-statistics, which supports the necessity for the consideration of structural break in M&A investigations. The growing trend of the M&A market in the emerging country described in Kale (2004) depicts that the M&A market was virtually nonexistent before the 1990s, however, the gradual financial liberalization attracts a rapid growth of participants.

In summary, the widely accepted view on the value destruction of M&A in developed nations appears uncertain in emerging countries, as existing theories and evidence are inconsistent. Some factors affecting acquisition performance such as ownership structure, government involvement, and institutional and corporate governance development in emerging countries behave differently in a different setting, which makes the answer on long-term wealth effects less predictable in the emerging world.

3. Data and Methodology

3.1. Data

3.1.1. Data Sources

The M&A events from emerging to developed countries are collected from the Thomson One database, for 20 years, from 1990 to 2010, a period right before the dawn of Industry 4.0. The data include characteristics of the deal, country, and industry specifics. Initially, the total number of M&A deals reach nearly 140,000. However, the final sample drops to 281 after screening out all the missing data (as shown in Table 1 and Figure 1). To compensate for the lack of recent data on M&As, firm specifics and return data are extracted from World Scope, thereby each acquiring firm is matched against a whole set of all available listed firms in the corresponding country. For example, to find the wealth effects of a cross-border M&A for each Indian acquirer, we collect from WorldScope the data on size, market-to-book, and cash holding level along with Datastream's return indices of all non-acquirer listed firms in India (more than 5000 firms) in the following five years to yield the optimal result. The total non-acquiring firms used for matching across the sample is 35,651, which makes our sample larger than most samples documented in the literature. These steps are carried out together with 20 years of data on M&A to ensure the reliability and representativeness of the wave of M&As from emerging to developed markets explored in this paper.

Table 1. Full sample overview.

Target Country	Acquirer Country	Number of Deals
All	All	139,895
All	Emerging	13,991
Developed	Emerging	1130
Developed	Emerging	281 *

* 281 is the final sample after screening out the missing data.

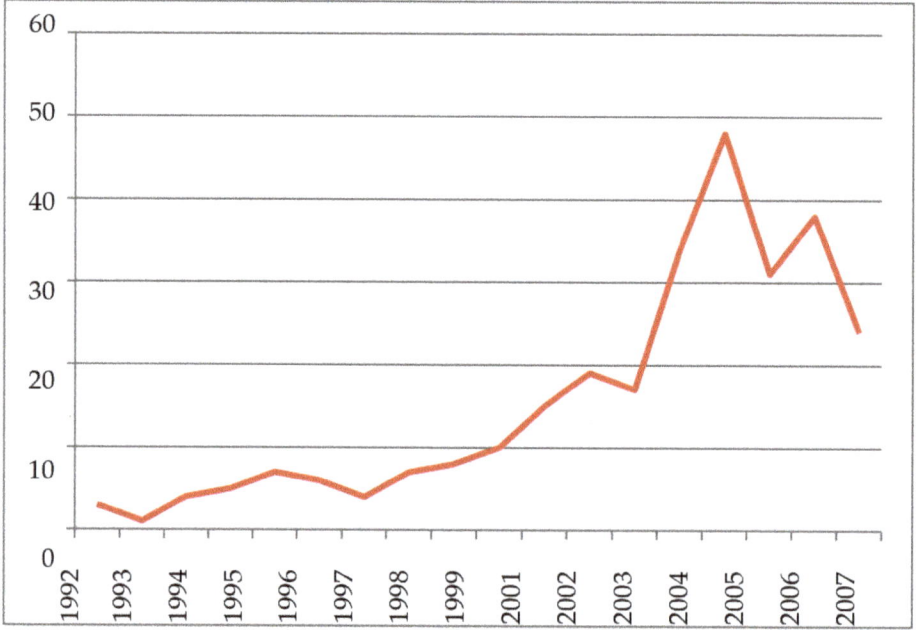

Figure 1. Number of deals by year (Source: study sample).

3.1.2. Sample Description

This section goes into a detailed description of the sample. The breakdown of the sample by emerging and developed countries shown in Table 2 illustrates that India is the most active country in CBMA to developed countries, while the U.S. is the top receiving country, as expected. Outbound M&A from an emerging to a developed country is a new trend, as less than 15 deals have been reported every single year until 2000. The frequency starts to pick up rapidly after 2000 and reaches a peak in 2008. A year after that, deals dropped dramatically, perhaps due to the financial crisis, which supports a view of structure break. Table 3 illustrates more details of the sample structure. It is noted that non-cash payment is dominant to cash payment, even though non-cash payments, as discussed earlier, imply ex-post underperformance. Other than that, the sample structure is consistent with our expectation. More specifically, related acquisition, acquisition for control, and inexperienced bidder are all dominant forces.

Table 2. Distribution of merger and acquisition (M&A) events by country (Source: authors' calculations).

Bidder Country	Frequency	Percent	Target Country	Frequency	Percent
India	96	34.16	USA	86	30.6
Malaysia	51	18.15	UK	52	18.51
South Africa	34	12.1	Australia	47	16.73
Taiwan	25	8.9	Canada	17	6.05
China	20	7.12	Germany	15	5.34
Russia	8	2.85	Italy	10	3.56
Mexico	7	2.49	Netherlands	7	2.49
Philippines	6	2.14	Japan	6	2.14
Poland	6	2.14	Spain	6	2.14
Korea	5	1.78	Denmark	4	1.42
Brazil	4	1.42	Finland	4	1.42
Egypt	3	1.07	Swiss	4	1.42
Hungary	3	1.07	Austria	3	1.07
Thailand	3	1.07	Belgium	3	1.07
Turkey	3	1.07	France	3	1.07
Argentina	2	0.71	Norway	3	1.07
Columbia	2	0.71	Sweden	3	1.07
Indonesia	1	0.36	Iceland	2	0.71
Pakistan	1	0.36	Luxembourg	2	0.71
Peru	1	0.36	Portugal	2	0.71
Total	281	100	Ireland	1	0.36
			New Zealand	1	0.36
			Total	281	100

Table 3. Breakdown of the sample by categories.

Category	M&A Type	Freq.	Percent.
Relatedness	Related acquisition	155	55.16
	Conglomerate acquisition	126	44.84
Acquisition for control	Less than 50% of the target's shares acquired	75	27.47
	More than 50% of the target's shares acquired	198	72.53
Payment method	Cash payment only	114	40.57
	Non-cash payment	167	59.43
Prior acquisition experience	Inexperienced bidder	190	67.62
	Experienced bidder	91	32.38

3.2. Methodology

The long-term wealth effect is estimated with the propensity score matching (PSM) model in tandem with differences-in-differences (DIDs), a quasi-experimental method attempted to replicate "randomized trials" in scientific experiments (Guo and Fraser 2014; Rubin 2008). Essentially, the PSM framework finds a counterfactual firm based on an ex-ante set of specific characteristics. In this paper, we assume that firms sharing a similar size, market-to-book, and cash level are subject to the same propensity of undertaking a similar acquisition. Barber and Lyon (1997) advocates for size and market-to-book along with Loughran and Ritter (1995), Spiess and Affleck-Graves (1995), and Fama and French (1993), while Jensen (1986) argues that cash level is a crucial determinant of acquisition decision. Further, Bhaumik and Gregoriou (2010) argue that cash abundance could motivate Indian firms into detrimental acquisitions. Besides the three conditioning variables, we also control for country and industry fixed effects. The PSM model specification is presented in Equation (1).

$$Prob\ (Acquirer_i = 1) = \alpha_i + \beta_i X_i + \gamma_i + \delta_i + \varepsilon_i, \quad (1)$$

where

Prob (Acquier$_i$ = 1): The probability of an emerging-market firm engaging in CBMA in developed markets
X_i: Three vectors representing the size, market-to-book, and cash level
γ_i: Control for country fixed effects
δ_i: Control for industry fixed effects
ε_i: The error term
α_i: The intercept

Given its advantage of multidimensional matching, the PSM alone is under scrutiny because it fails to account for the longitudinal nature of the sample where the return is observed at two different time stamps (Heckman et al. 1997). Thus, it needs to coordinate with DIDs to cope with the dynamics of the event study, thereby capable of reducing selections on observables and *"temporal time-invariant"* unobservables (Guo and Fraser 2014; Girma et al. 2006; and Blundell and Dias 2000). The final estimator is given in Equation (2).

$$DIDs = \frac{1}{n_1} \sum_{i \in T}^{n_1} \left[(Y_{1t_1 i} - Y_{1t_0 i}) - \sum_{j \in C}^{n_2} W(i,j)(Y_{0t_1 j} - Y_{0t_0 j}) \right], \qquad (2)$$

where

DIDs: The estimated long-term wealth effect
$T = \{i_1, i_2, \ldots, i_{n_1}\}$: The set of acquirers
$C = \{j_1, j_2, \ldots, j_{n_2}\}$: The set of counterfactual firms
(Y_1, Y_0): The respective observed return of the acquirer, and its counterfactual
(t_0, t_1): Lower bound and upper bound of the event window
$(Y_{1t_1 i} - Y_{1t_0 i})$: The observed return growth of the acquirer in the event window
$(Y_{0t_1 j} - Y_{0t_0 j})$: The observed return growth of a control firm in the event window
$W(i,j)$: The Kernel weighting function
$\sum_{j \in C}^{n_2} W(i,j)(Y_{0t_1 j} - Y_{0t_0 j})$: The estimated counterfactual return growth

The weighting kernel function allows for one-to-many matching under two conditions: (1) the counterfactual's propensity falls within a certain radius of acquirer's, and (2) the acquirer and control firms must be in the same common support region to ensure a match for each acquirer. With the kernel-based matching mechanism (KBM), the control firm within the radius will be assigned higher weight if its propensity is closer to that of the acquirer. Moreover, trimming levels of 2%, 5%, and 10% are undertaken as a sensitivity check for the acquirer and controls stay within the common support region, a procedure suggested by Heckman et al. (1997) and Guo and Fraser (2014).

In summary, this paper employs PSM and DIDs to estimate the long-run wealth effect, given its advantages in dealing with selections on both observables (e.g., size, market-to-book, and cash level) as well as "temporal time-invariant" unobservables. Such advantages are significant as "the power of event study methodology depends crucially on the quality of the benchmark" (Dimson and Marsh 1986).

4. Results and Discussion

4.1. Full Sample Analysis

The DIDs' estimates illustrate significant negative wealth effects in the course of three, four, and five years after the effective date of the CBMA transaction, and the evidence is consistent for all sensitivity analyses on a 2%, 5%, and 10% trimming level. Table 4 clearly shows a higher detrimental effect when the event window is longer. The abnormal return is around 26% in the three-year window but could reach more than 70% in a five-year window. Thus, if the non-acquirer's stock return stays unchanged, the acquirer's relatively goes down by 26% after three years and down by approximately 70% after five years. The manifested evidence is strong, but not uncanny in the literature. For example, Agrawal et al. (1992) find that acquirers underperform by 10.26% in a six-year event window, while Sudarsanam and Gao (2003) report 32% underperformance of U.K. high-tech firms in just a one-year event window. Conn et al. (2005) also find a decrease of 19.78% in a three-year event window. The strong evidence of detrimental wealth effect indicates that the potential synergies in CBMA from emerging to developed nations have never been materialized, or the relating frictions outweigh the synergies of the M&A in the long run.

4.2. Subsample Analysis

Further examination of subsamples based on potential factors underpinning the wealth effect demonstrates consistent negative wealth effects across the results (Table 4, Panel B). Related acquisition underperforms by 46.18% to 50.84% after four years, while unrelated acquisition underperforms after five years, ranging from 50.76% to 57.79%. This evidence is not aligned with the prior expectation that either related or unrelated may provide incremental wealth effects.

Also, this paper anticipates that the negative effect may be different in consideration of the payment method. However, we find no evidence of positive long-term adjustment. Moreover, the non-cash demonstrates a powerful value destruction effect after three and especially five years. Specifically, if the return of a counterfactual group increases by 100%, such a return of the acquirer with non-cash financing increases about 10% at best or possibly stays the same after five years. Such strong evidence lends support to the signaling theory because no significant negative abnormal return is observed in the cash-financing subsample.

Furthermore, the power of control is unable to overwhelm the overall negative effect, because significant underperformance evidence is observed in the three- to five-year windows. The level of negative in this subsample is similar to that in the full sample, indicating that taming of the incomplete contract issues or control of strategic assets is insufficient to defeat the post-integration problems.

Finally, similar stories unfold for the experience and the structure break. No sign of positive effects is reported, which again highlights the predominance of ex-post integration issues over acquirer's experience. Similarly, positive change in the business environment during the second period of the merger is not yet adequate to create a positive effect.

Overall, we find strong evidence of the bidder's long-term value destruction in all settings, which is consistent with the previous literature. However, the special finding is that a variety of potential factors previously shown to be capable of undermining difficulties in M&A were all rendered ineffective.

Table 4. Full sample and subsample results.

Sample	Event Window	Spec 1	Spec 2	Spec 3
	Panel A: Full sample			
	1	−0.0095	−0.0080	−0.0018
	2	−0.0711	−0.0774	−0.0714
	3	−0.2613 **	−0.2806 **	−0.2592 **
	4	−0.3680 **	−0.3970 **	−0.3538 **
	5	−0.6914 **	−0.7141 **	−0.6167 **
	Panel B: Acquirers with no prior experience in developed markets			
No Exp.	1	−0.0276	−0.0287	−0.0287
	2	−0.0875	−0.1063	−0.1063
	3	−0.2354	−0.2506	−0.2506
	4	−0.3992 **	−0.4261 **	−0.4261 **
	5	−0.7816 **	−0.8156 **	−0.8156 **

Table 4. *Cont.*

Sample	Event Window	Spec 1	Spec 2	Spec 3
Panel C: Related vs. Unrelated				
Related	1	−0.1279	−0.1310	−0.1221
	2	−0.1684	−0.1751	−0.1716
	3	−0.2954	−0.3291	−0.2984
	4	−0.4730 **	−0.5084 **	−0.4618 **
	5	−0.7535	−0.7681	−0.7163
Unrelated	1	0.0867	0.0868	0.0792
	2	0.0029	0.0088	0.0161
	3	−0.2250	−0.2282	−0.2156
	4	−0.2801	−0.2709	−0.2428
	5	−0.5779 **	−0.5718 **	−0.5076 **
Panel D: Acquisitions NOT funded by pure cash				
Non-Cash	1	0.0092	−0.0056	0.0103
	2	−0.0866	−0.1029	−0.0867
	3	−0.3983 **	−0.4259 **	−0.3907 **
	4	−0.5369	−0.5415	−0.4886
	5	−0.9869 **	−0.9705 **	−0.8913 **
Panel E: Acquisitions for control				
Control 50	1	−0.0488	−0.0577	−0.0426
	2	−0.1158	−0.1271	−0.1187
	3	−0.3370 **	−0.3688 **	−0.3464 **
	4	−0.3671 **	−0.3960 **	−0.3753 **
	5	−0.6675 **	−0.6703 **	−0.6148 **
Minority	1	0.0783	0.0963	0.0909
	2	0.0144	0.0260	0.0237
	3	−0.0251	−0.0085	−0.0388
	4	−0.2926	−0.2873	−0.2897
	5	−0.6105 **	−0.6256 **	−0.6242 **
Panel F: Acquisitions in two merger waves				
Before 2003	1	−0.0034	−0.0007	0.0220
	2	−0.0901	−0.1092	−0.0874
	3	−0.3129 **	−0.3513 **	−0.3359 **
	4	−0.4541 **	−0.5226 **	−0.4589 **
	5	−0.7514 **	−0.8739 **	−0.7366 **
After 2003	1	−0.0192	−0.0214	−0.0168
	2	−0.0780	−0.0867	−0.0882
	3	−0.2481	−0.2844	−0.2703
	4	−0.3418 **	−0.3790 **	−0.3664 **
	5	−0.6088 **	−0.6363 **	−0.5980 **

NOTE: The table reports the average treatment effects on the treated (i.e., wealth effect) in the long-run. Specification 1: The default setting where no trimming is made and bandwidth is set to 0.8. Specification 2: 5% of the treated cases are trimmed to drop cases in the off-support region. Specification 3: The bandwidth is set to a smaller value of 0.5, meaning that a smaller number of control cases is used in the calculation of the counterfactual outcome. ** significant at the 5% conventional level, generated by the bias-corrected (BC) method in the bootstrapping procedure.

5. Conclusions

This study sets out to examine the wealth effect of cross-border M&A from emerging to developed countries on the acquiring firm. Using a comprehensive sample from the 1990–2010 period, we find strong, statistically significant evidence for the negative wealth effects of M&A events. The negative wealth effects are consistently estimated in three-, four-, and five-year event windows, and reach approximately −69% after five years. This evidence highlights the difficulty to achieve synergies in cross-border M&As from emerging to advanced markets, in which, even a time window of five years, would not mitigate the negative effects. This result suggests conflicts that come from differences in culture, institution, market, business practice, and so on (Dunning et al. 2007; Gallo and Sveen 1991; Nguyen et al. 2019; Vuong 2016a, 2016b) present considerable challenges for emerging market acquirers to benefit from M&A deals in mature markets.

More importantly, this study finds that the negative effects remain persistent even when we control for factors presumed to have potentially positive impacts, such as industry relatedness, method of payment (Mitchell and Stafford 2000; Sudarsanam and Mahate 2003), acquisition for control (Cosh and Guest 2001; Franks and Harris 1989), prior experience (Aggarwal and Samwick 2003; Barkema et al. 1996), and structure break (Jarrell and Bradley 1980). We find that M&A with the non-cash financing method show a strong negative wealth effect after three and five years. This observation lends support to the signaling theory (Connelly et al. 2011) that no significant negative abnormal return is revealed in the cash-financing subsample. Furthermore, our study shows the power to control, especially to mitigate the negative impacts of an incomplete contract, or the ability to control strategic assets are not enough to overcome the post-merger problems (Agrawal et al. 1992; Rau and Vermaelen 1998). As for the structure break and prior experience aspects, the analyses indicate similar trends: there is no statistical evidence for positive effects. This result sheds light on the predominance of post-acquisition issues over acquirer's experience and favorable changes in business environment during the second period of the merger.

Our strong evidence highlights the remarkable nature of value destruction of inter-country M&A investments from the emerging to the developed world, which could serve to admonish companies in emerging countries to consider their future M&As deals in advanced markets more carefully.

Future research could choose a particular factor to focus on or replicate the study in a more recent period. As the analysis is based on key assumptions such as "bigger is better," "heavy bureaucracy," and dominance of state control in big companies, the results are bound to change if these assumptions change. Another suggestion is to cover further analysis using Bayesian network modeling with the "bayesvl" R package (La and Vuong 2019; Vuong and La 2019). Last, but not least, with the arrival of Industry 4.0 and the rapid change of globalization, the landscape of entrepreneurial finance has shifted remarkably, especially for emerging markets (Block et al. 2018; Nguyen et al. 2019). This shifting business landscape can lead to new findings and possibly positive long-run performance for firms engaged in cross-border M&A. As such, future studies should extend the research period to cover more recent events; further scientific understanding in this area will be vital to prevent policy failure (Vuong 2018; Vuong et al. 2019).

Author Contributions: Conceptualization, H.-H.H. and T.-H.V.; methodology, N.-T.D.; software, Q.-H.V.; validation, Q.-H.V. and M.-T.H.; formal analysis, N.-T.D. and M.-T.H.; investigation, H.-H.H.; resources, T.-H.V.; data curation, H.-H.H., T.-H.V., and N.-T.D.; writing—original draft preparation, H.-H.H. and M.-T.H.; writing—review and editing, Q.-H.V. and M.-T.H.; supervision, Q.-H.V.; project administration, Q.-H.V. and T.-H.V.; funding acquisition, T.-H.V.

Funding: This research is sponsored by Foreign Trade University under the project "Political and Social aspects of Vietnam's international integration.

Conflicts of Interest: The authors declare no conflict of interest.

References

Aggarwal, Rajesh K., and Andrew A. Samwick. 2003. Why do managers diversify their firms? Agency reconsidered. *The Journal of Finance* 58: 71–118. [CrossRef]

Agrawal, Anup, Jeffrey F. Jaffe, and Gershon N. Mandelker. 1992. The post-merger performance of acquiring firms: A re-examination of an anomaly. *The Journal of Finance* 47: 1605–21. [CrossRef]

Agudelo, Diego A., Santiago Giraldo, and Edwin Villarraga. 2015. Does PIN measure information? Informed trading effects on returns and liquidity in six emerging markets. *International Review of Economics & Finance* 39: 149–61.

Al Rahahleh, Naseem, and Peihwang Philip Wei. 2012. The performance of frequent acquirers: Evidence from emerging markets. *Global Finance Journal* 23: 16–33. [CrossRef]

Antkiewicz, Agata, and John Whalley. 2006. Recent Chinese buyout activity and the implications for global architecture. In *NBER Working Paper No. 12072*. NBER Program(s). Boston, U.S.: National Bureau of Economic Research. Available online: https://www.nber.org/papers/w12072.pdf (accessed on 19 June 2019).

Asquith, Paul, Robert F. Bruner, and David W. Mullins. 1983. The gains to bidding firms from merger. *Journal of Financial Economics* 11: 121–39. [CrossRef]

Barber, Brad M., and John D. Lyon. 1997. Detecting long-run abnormal stock returns: The empirical power and specification of test statistics. *Journal of Financial Economics* 43: 341–72. [CrossRef]

Barkema, Harry G., John H. J. Bell, and Johannes M. Pennings. 1996. Foreign entry, cultural barriers, and learning. *Strategic Management Journal* 17: 151–66. [CrossRef]

Bhabra, Harjeet S., and Jiayin Huang. 2013. An empirical investigation of mergers and acquisitions by Chinese listed companies, 1997–2007. *Journal of Multinational Financial Management* 23: 186–207. [CrossRef]

Bhagat, Sanjai, Andrei Shleifer, Robert W. Vishny, Gregg Jarrel, and Lawrence Summers. 1990. Hostile takeovers in the 1980s: The return to corporate specialization. *Brookings Papers on Economic Activity. Microeconomics* 1990: 1–84. [CrossRef]

Bhaumik, Sumon Kumar, and Nigel Driffield. 2011. Direction of outward FDI of EMNEs: Evidence from the Indian pharmaceutical sector. *Thunderbird International Business Review* 53: 615–28. [CrossRef]

Bhaumik, Sumon Kumar, and Andros Gregoriou. 2010. 'Family' ownership, tunnelling and earnings management: A review of the literature. *Journal of Economic Surveys* 24: 705–30. [CrossRef]

Block, Joern H., Massimo G. Colombo, Douglas J. Cumming, and Silvio Vismara. 2018. New players in entrepreneurial finance and why they are there. *Small Business Economics* 50: 239–50. [CrossRef]

Blundell, Richard, and Monica Costa Dias. 2000. Evaluation methods for non-experimental data. *Fiscal Studies* 21: 427–68. [CrossRef]

Boateng, Agyenim, and Wei Huang. 2017. Multiple large shareholders, excess leverage and tunneling: Evidence from an emerging market. *Corporate Governance: An International Review* 25: 58–74. [CrossRef]

Bradley, Michael, and Anant Sundaram. 2004. Do Acquisitions Drive Performance or Does Performance Drive Acquisitions? Available online: https://www.researchgate.net/publication/272248116_Do_Acquisitions_Drive_Performance_or_Does_Performance_Drive_Acquisitions (accessed on 28 May 2019).

Campa, Jose Manuel, and Simi Kedia. 2002. Explaining the diversification discount. *The Journal of Finance* 57: 1731–62. [CrossRef]

Chari, Anusha, Paige P. Ouimet, and Linda L. Tesar. 2009. The value of control in emerging markets. *Review of Financial Studies* 23: 1741–70. [CrossRef]

Chevalier, Judith. 2004. What do we know about cross-subsidization? Evidence from merging firms. *Advances in Economic Analysis & Policy* 4. [CrossRef]

Cogman, David, Patrick Jaslowitzer, and Marc Steffen Rap. 2015. Why Emerging-Market Companies Acquire Abroad. Available online: https://www.mckinsey.com/~{}/media/McKinsey/dotcom/client_service/Corporate%20Finance/MoF/Issue%2055/MoF55_Why_emerging-market_companies_acquire_abroad.ashx (accessed on 29 May 2019).

Comment, Robert, and Gregg A. Jarrell. 1995. Corporate focus and stock returns. *Journal of Financial Economics* 37: 67–87. [CrossRef]

Conn, Robert L., Andy Cosh, Paul M. Guest, and Alan Hughes. 2005. The impact on UK acquirers of domestic, cross-border, public and private acquisitions. *Journal of Business Finance & Accounting* 32: 815–70. [CrossRef]

Connelly, Brian L., S. Trevis Certo, R. Duane Ireland, and Christopher R. Reutzel. 2011. Signaling theory: A review and assessment. *Journal of Management* 37: 39–67. [CrossRef]

Cosh, Andy, and Paul Guest. 2001. The Long-Run Performance of Hostile Takeovers: UK Evidence. Available online: http://www.cbr.cam.ac.uk/fileadmin/user_upload/centre-for-business-research/downloads/working-papers/wp215.pdf (accessed on 28 May 2019).

Deng, Ping. 2004. Outward investment by Chinese MNCs: Motivations and implications. *Business Horizons* 47: 8–16. [CrossRef]

Deng, Ping. 2013. Chinese outward direct investment research: Theoretical integration and recommendations. *Management and Organization Review* 9: 513–39. [CrossRef]

Deng, Ping, and Monica Yang. 2015. Cross-border mergers and acquisitions by emerging market firms: A comparative investigation. *International Business Review* 24: 157–72. [CrossRef]

Dimson, Elroy, and Paul Marsh. 1986. Event study methodologies and the size effect. *Journal of Financial Economics* 17: 113–42. [CrossRef]

Dunning, John H., Yong Suhk Pak, and Sam Beldona. 2007. Foreign ownership strategies of UK and US intersnational franchisors: An exploratory application of Dunning's envelope paradigm. *International Business Review* 16: 531–48. [CrossRef]

Dyck, Alexander, and Luigi Zingales. 2004. Private benefits of control: An international comparison. *The Journal of Finance* 59: 537–600. [CrossRef]

Faccio, Mara. 2010. Differences between politically connected and nonconnected firms: A cross-country analysis. *Financial Management* 39: 905–28. [CrossRef]

Fama, Eugene F., and Kenneth R. French. 1993. Common risk factors in the returns on stocks and bonds. *Journal of Financial Economics* 33: 3–56. [CrossRef]

Franks, Julian R., and Robert S. Harris. 1989. Shareholder wealth effects of corporate takeovers. *Journal of Financial Economics* 23: 225–49. [CrossRef]

Gallo, Miguel Angel, and Jannicke Sveen. 1991. Internationalizing the family business: Facilitating and restraining factors. *Family Business Review* 4: 181–90. [CrossRef]

Gatzer, Sebastian, Daniel Hoang, and Martin Ruckes. 2014. *Internal Capital Markets and Diversified Firms: Theory and Practice*. KIT Working Paper Series in Economics, No. 64. Karlsruhe: Karlsruher Institut für Technologie (KIT), Available online: https://www.econstor.eu/bitstream/10419/104706/1/810608103.pdf (accessed on 19 June 2019).

Gibson, Michael S. 2003. Is corporate governance ineffective in emerging markets? *Journal of Financial and Quantitative Analysis* 38: 231–50. [CrossRef]

Girma, Sourafel, David Greenaway, and Richard Kneller. 2003. Export market exit and performance dynamics: A causality analysis of matched firms. *Economics Letters* 80: 181–87. [CrossRef]

Girma, Sourafel, Steve Thompson, and Peter W. Wright. 2006. International acquisitions, domestic competition and firm performance. *International Journal of the Economics of Business* 13: 335–49. [CrossRef]

Graham, John R., Michael L. Lemmon, and Jack G. Wolf. 2002. Does corporate diversification destroy value? *The Journal of Finance* 57: 695–720. [CrossRef]

Grimpe, Christoph, and Katrin Hussinger. 2009. Building and Blocking: The Two Faces of Technology Acquisition pdf Logo. Available online: https://www.econstor.eu/handle/10419/27588 (accessed on 17 June 2019).

Grossman, Sanford J., and Oliver D. Hart. 1986. The costs and benefits of ownership: A theory of vertical and lateral integration. *Journal of Political Economy* 94: 691–719. [CrossRef]

Guillén, Mauro F., and Esteban García-Canal. 2009. The American model of the multinational firm and the "new" multinationals from emerging economies. *Academy of Management Perspectives* 23: 23–35. [CrossRef]

Guo, Shenyang, and Mark W. Fraser. 2014. *Propensity Score Analysis: Statistical Methods and Applications*. London: Sage.

Heckman, James J., Hidehiko Ichimura, and Petra E. Todd. 1997. Matching as an econometric evaluation estimator: Evidence from evaluating a job training programme. *The Review of Economic Studies* 64: 605–54. [CrossRef]

Jarrell, Gregg A., and Michael Bradley. 1980. The economic effects of federal and state regulations of cash tender offers. *The Journal of Law and Economics* 23: 371–407. [CrossRef]

Jensen, Michael C. 1986. Agency costs of free cash flow, corporate finance, and takeovers. *The American Economic Review* 76: 323–29.

Jensen, Michael C., and William H. Meckling. 1976. Theory of the firm: Managerial behavior, agency costs and ownership structure. *Journal of Financial Economics* 3: 305–60. [CrossRef]

Jensen, Michael C., and Richard S. Ruback. 1983. The market for corporate control. *Journal of Financial Economics* 11: 5–50. [CrossRef]

Kale, Prashant. 2004. Acquisition value creation in emerging markets: An empirical study of acquisitions in India. *Academy of Management Proceedings* 2004: H1–H6. [CrossRef]

Khanna, Tarun, and Krishna Palepu. 2000. Is group affiliation profitable in emerging markets? An analysis of diversified Indian business groups. *The Journal of Finance* 55: 867–91. [CrossRef]

La, V. P., and Q. H. Vuong. 2019. Bayesvl: Visually Learning the Graphical Structure of Bayesian Networks and Performing MCMC with 'Stan'. The Comprehensive R Archive Network (CRAN). Version 0.8.5. Available online: https://cran.r-project.org/web/packages/bayesvl/index.html (accessed on 24 May 2019).

Lang, Larry H. P., and Rene M. Stulz. 1994. Tobin's q, corporate diversification, and firm performance. *Journal of Political Economy* 102: 1248–80.

Lebedev, Sergey, Mike W. Peng, En Xie, and Charles E. Stevens. 2015. Mergers and acquisitions in and out of emerging economies. *Journal of World Business* 50: 651–62. [CrossRef]

Lien, Lasse B., and Peter G. Klein. 2008. Using competition to measure relatedness. *Journal of Management* 35: 1078–107. [CrossRef]

Loughran, Tim, and Jay R. Ritter. 1995. The new issues puzzle. *The Journal of Finance* 50: 23–51. [CrossRef]

Loughran, Tim, and Anand M. Vijh. 1997. Do long-term shareholders benefit from corporate acquisitions? *The Journal of Finance* 52: 1765–90. [CrossRef]

Luo, Yadong. 2001. Determinants of entry in an emerging economy: A multilevel approach. *Journal of Management Studies* 38: 443–72. [CrossRef]

Martynova, Marina, and Luc Renneboog. 2009. What determines the financing decision in corporate takeovers: Cost of capital, agency problems, or the means of payment? *Journal of Corporate Finance* 15: 290–315. [CrossRef]

Matsusaka, John G., and Vikram Nanda. 2002. Internal capital markets and corporate refocusing. *Journal of Financial Intermediation* 11: 176–211. [CrossRef]

Mitchell, Mark L., and Erik Stafford. 2000. Managerial decisions and long-term stock price performance. *The Journal of Business* 73: 287–329. [CrossRef]

Myers, Stewart C., and Nicholas S. Majluf. 1984. Corporate financing and investment decisions when firms have information that investors do not have. *Journal of Financial Economics* 13: 187–221. [CrossRef]

Nguyen, To Hong-Kong, To Viet-Ha Nguyen, Thu-Trang Vuong, Manh-Tung Ho, and Quan-Hoang Vuong. 2019. The new politics of debt in the transition economy of Vietnam. *Austrian Journal of South-East Asian Studies* 12: 91–109. [CrossRef]

O'Hara, Maureen. 2003. Presidential address: Liquidity and price discovery. *The Journal of Finance* 58: 1335–54. [CrossRef]

OECD. 2017. Cross-Border M&A on the Rise. Available online: https://www.oecd.org/investment/globalforum/2017-GFII-Background-Note-MA-trends.pdf (accessed on 29 May 2017).

Radelet, Steven, Jeffrey D. Sachs, Richard N. Cooper, and Barry P. Bosworth. 1998. The East Asian financial crisis: Diagnosis, remedies, prospects. *Brookings Papers on Economic Activity* 1998: 1–90. [CrossRef]

Rau, P. Raghavendra, and Theo Vermaelen. 1998. Glamour, value and the post-acquisition performance of acquiring firms. *Journal of Financial Economics* 49: 223–53.

Roll, Richard. 1986. The hubris hypothesis of corporate takeovers. *Journal of Business* 59: 197–216. [CrossRef]

Rubin, Donald B. 2008. For objective causal inference, design trumps analysis. *The Annals of Applied Statistics* 2: 808–40. [CrossRef]

Scharfstein, David S., and Jeremy C. Stein. 2000. The dark side of internal capital markets: Divisional rent-seeking and inefficient investment. *The Journal of Finance* 55: 2537–64. [CrossRef]

Servaes, Henri. 1996. The value of diversification during the conglomerate merger wave. *The Journal of Finance* 51: 1201–25. [CrossRef]

Sheng, Shibin, Kevin Zheng Zhou, and Julie Juan Li. 2011. The effects of business and political ties on firm performance: Evidence from China. *Journal of Marketing* 75: 1–15. [CrossRef]

Spiess, D. Katherine, and John Affleck-Graves. 1995. Underperformance in long-run stock returns following seasoned equity offerings. *Journal of Financial Economics* 38: 243–67. [CrossRef]

Stein, Jeremy C. 2003. Chapter 2—Agency, Information and Corporate Investment. In *Handbook of the Economics of Finance*. Edited by George M. Constantinides, Milton Harris and René M. Stulz. Amsterdam: Elsevier, pp. 111–65.

Stulz, René M. 1990. Managerial discretion and optimal financing policies. *Journal of Financial Economics* 26: 3–27. [CrossRef]

Sudarsanam, Puliyur, and Lin Gao. 2003. *Value Creation in UK High Technology Acquisitions*. EFMA 2004 Basel Meetings Paper. Available online: https://ssrn.com/abstract=493762 (accessed on 19 June 2019). [CrossRef]

Sudarsanam, Sudi, and Ashraf A. Mahate. 2003. Glamour acquirers, method of payment and post-acquisition performance: The UK evidence. *Journal of Business Finance & Accounting* 30: 299–342.

Sun, Pei, Kamel Mellahi, and Mike Wright. 2012. The contingent value of corporate political ties. *Academy of Management Perspectives* 26: 68–82. [CrossRef]

Tanna, Sailesh, and Ibrahim Yousef. 2019. Mergers and acquisitions: Implications for acquirers' market risk. *Managerial Finance* 45: 545–62. [CrossRef]

UNCTAD. 2014. Investing in the SDGs: An Action Plan. Available online: https://unctad.org/en/PublicationsLibrary/wir2014_en.pdf (accessed on 29 May 2019).

Villalonga, Belén. 2004. Does diversification cause the "diversification discount"? *Financial Management* 33: 5–27. [CrossRef]

Vuong, Quan Hoang. 2016a. Determinants of firm performance in a less innovative transition system: Exploring Vietnamese longitudinal data. *International Journal of Transitions and Innovation Systems* 5: 20–45. [CrossRef]

Vuong, Quan-Hoang. 2016b. Impacts of geographical locations and sociocultural traits on the Vietnamese entrepreneurship. *SpringerPlus* 5: 1189. [CrossRef]

Vuong, Quan-Hoang. 2018. The (ir)rational consideration of the cost of science in transition economies. *Nature Human Behaviour* 2: 5. [CrossRef] [PubMed]

Vuong, Quan-Hoang. 2019. Computational entrepreneurship: From economic complexities to interdisciplinary research. *Problems and Perspectives in Management* 17: 117–29. [CrossRef]

Vuong, Quan Hoang, and Viet Phuong La. 2019. BayesVL Package for Bayesian Statistical analyses in R. Github. v0.8.5. Available online: https://github.com/sshpa/bayesvl (accessed on 17 June 2019). [CrossRef]

Vuong, Quan-Hoang, Thu-Trang Vuong, To Hong-Kong Nguyen, and Manh-Tung Ho. 2019. The "same bed, different dreams" of Vietnam and China: How (mis)trust could make or break it. *European Journal of East Asian Studies* 18: 1–36. [CrossRef]

Young, Michael N., Mike W. Peng, David Ahlstrom, Garry D. Bruton, and Yi Jiang. 2008. Corporate governance in emerging economies: A review of the principal–principal perspective. *Journal of Management Studies* 45: 196–220. [CrossRef]

© 2019 by the authors. Licensee MDPI, Basel, Switzerland. This article is an open access article distributed under the terms and conditions of the Creative Commons Attribution (CC BY) license (http://creativecommons.org/licenses/by/4.0/).

Article

Adaptive Market Hypothesis: Evidence from the Vietnamese Stock Market

Dzung Phan Tran Trung [1] and Hung Pham Quang [2,*]

[1] Faculty of Banking & Finance, Foreign Trade University, Hanoi 100000, Vietnam; fandzung@ftu.edu.vn
[2] Branch of PwC (Vietnam) Limited in Hanoi, Hanoi 100000, Vietnam
* Correspondence: hungqp.k53@ftu.edu.vn; Tel.: +84-383-351-868

Received: 30 March 2019; Accepted: 5 May 2019; Published: 8 May 2019

Abstract: This paper aims to test the adaptive market hypothesis in the two main Vietnamese stock exchanges, namely Ho Chi Minh City Stock Exchange (HSX) and Hanoi Stock Exchange (HNX), by measuring the relationship between current stock returns and historical stock returns. In particular, the tests employed are the automatic variance ratio test ("AVR"), the automatic portmanteau test ("AP"), the generalized spectral test ("GS"), and the time-varying autoregressive (TV-AR) approach. The empirical results validate the adaptive market hypothesis in the Vietnamese stock market. Furthermore, the results suggest that the evolution of HSX has served as an important factor of the adaptive market hypothesis.

Keywords: adaptive market hypothesis; market efficiency; autocorrelation

1. Introduction

Efficient market hypothesis (EMH), proposed by Fama (1970), despite being well known and influential in finance theory and practice, is still controversial in the predictability of stock market return. A strong and still rising school of theory, behavioral finance, is one of the strongest opponents against the arguments of EMH. The core question to this debate is whether stock market movements are predictable. The idea for the adaptive market hypothesis (AMH) stemmed from the reasoning of Lo (2004), which claimed much of evidence of an investor's irrationality (e.g., loss aversion, overconfidence, overreaction) is, in fact, consistent with the evolutionary model of human behaviors. Such an evolutionary model indicates that humans adaptation to the ever-changing surroundings is a result of their continuous perception and learning of the latter. This evolutionary model is further developed into the adaptive market hypothesis (Lo 2004). Lo (2005) states "Based on evolutionary principles, the adaptive market hypothesis implies that the degree of market efficiency is related to environmental factors characterizing market ecologies such as the number of competitors in the market, the magnitude of profit opportunities available, and the adaptability of the market participants." The key point for AMH to be the harmonization of EMH and BF is investor's ability to learn and to adapt to the market's updated situation, as a result, financial markets can be wrong from time to time, but they learned, evolved to be right, until the next mistake. Cyclical repeats of market inefficiency are the sign of adaptation, according to AMH. Since its emergence, the AMH theory has drawn significant attention from academic researchers.

1.1. Papers Discussing Adaptive Market Hypothesis (AMH)

In expansion to Lo's work (2004), Lim and Brooks (2011) proposed two criteria to test the AMH theory:

- The market efficiency should be varying through time;

- The market efficiency should be dependent on market conditions (i.e., financial crises, market crashes, stock bubbles, ...).

Most of the evidences found in existing literature conclude that the AMH theory describes the fluctuations of stock returns better that the EMH theory. Specifically, interesting findings about overtime changes of market efficiency are clearly seen in the studies of Lim et al. (2006) examining the cases of in developed and emerging countries and Ito and Sugiyama (2009) researching the phenomenon of time-varying autocorrelation of the monthly S&P 500 stock returns.

Neely et al. (2009) studied the intertemporal stability of excess returns to technical trading rules in the foreign exchange market by conducting true, out-of-sample tests on previously studied rules. They found that excess returns were genuine in the 1970s and 1980s, but gradually declined in the 1990s. This result was consistent with the AMH framework.

Kim et al. (2011) examined the AMH theory by testing the feasibility of stock return forecast, using the daily and weekly Dow Jones Industrial Average (DJIA) stock returns from 1900 to 2009. They discovered that in the case where current stock returns can be accurately predicted using historical prices, the market efficiency is low. Kim employed three autocorrelation tests, which were the variance ratio test, portmanteau test and the generalized spectral (GS) test to measure the significance of the autocorrelation. The results indicate that the autocorrelation significance in the data series fluctuated over time and was dependent on the market conditions. Regarding the market condition dependency, the market is efficient in times of market crashes, however, it is inefficient in times of crises.

Smith (2012) tested the AMH theory in 15 stock markets of emerging European countries with those of more developed ones, such as Greece, Portugal, and United England. The variance ratio test is conducted on the time series data from February 2000 to December 2009. The results show that market efficiency changes over time to some extent, which is consistent with the AMH theory.

Lim et al. (2013) found that in large US stock indices, the degree of market efficiency expressed volatility over time. The study applies autocorrelation tests on a rolling-window basis. Additionally, the bootstrapping procedure was also used to make conclusions. Their main finding is that the studied market went through multiple periods of efficiency and periods of inefficiency.

Urquhart and McGroarty (2014) tested the adaptive market hypothesis through four well-known calendar anomalies in the Dow Jones Industrial Average from 1900 to 2013 using subsample analysis and rolling window analysis. The results showed that all four calendar anomalies support the AMH, with each calendar anomaly's performance varying over time. They concluded that the AMH provides a better explanation for calendar anomalies than the EMH.

Hiremath and Kumari (2014) employed linear and non-linear methods to test the cyclical phenomenon in India's stock market. They found that with the linear method the Indian stock market showed a cyclical pattern, while this pattern was not found using the non-linear method.

Besides the statistical tests using the moving window method, another approach is also employed to measure market efficiency, i.e., the time-varying model approach.

Ito et al. (2014) applied a non-Bayesian time-varying vector autoregressive (TV-VAR) model to estimate the joint degree of market efficiency. Their results conclude that the international linkages and market efficiency change over time and that market behaviors correspond well to historical events of the international financial system.

Ito et al. (2016) applied TV-AR model to test the evolution through time of the U.S. stock market. The main findings show that (i) the U.S. market efficiency changes over time, and (ii) efficiency were violated during recessions, consistent with the assumption of behavioral finance.

Noda (2016) tested AMH within the Japanese context, the study employed a time-varying model approach, and concluded that the degree of market efficiency changes over time in the markets (TOPIX and TSE2), the evolving process of the market efficiency varies among stock markets, and the results support the AMH for the more qualified stock market in Japan.

Almost all of the aforementioned papers have the same finding, which is that the AMH theory describes fluctuations in stock prices more accurately than the EMH theory. Using two criteria proposed by Lim and Brooks (2011), some important aspects needed to take into consideration in this paper are: (1) the evolution through time of market, (2) applicability of AMH in different exchanges and (3) the connection between market efficiency and economic cycle.

1.2. Papers Discussing Vietnamese Stock Market Efficiency

The Viet Nam Stock Market (VSM) consists of two stock exchanges: Ho Chi Minh stock exchange (HOSE) and Hanoi Stock Exchange (HNX) and the VSM performs better now than in the pre-World Trade Organization (WTO) period in terms of both initial public offerings (IPOs) and seasoned offerings (Vuong 2018). Vietnamese stock market, despite having a great opportunity to have an upgraded status from frontier market to emerging market by Morgan Stanley Capital International (MSCI) in the near future, still faces with many potential issues regarding efficiency due to its special characteristics especially in the age of digitization and globalization, listed companies worldwide particularly are facing increasing pressure to innovate, increase productivity and increase competitiveness (Vu et al. 2019). Efficiency is, therefore, of the utmost importance to firms and markets as well. With 19 years of existence, the market has gone through different phases, from almost inactive in the first 5 years, then a boom and burst in the next 3 years, and unstable status with different ups and downs afterward until the moment when speed is everything: Speed of calculation, the speed of thinking, the speed of failing (Vuong 2019). There is a constant pressure to keep up the streams of content and investors tend to make decisions based on external information of quotations on the stock market. Apart from that, the number of institutional investors and foreign investors in the Vietnamese stock market is approximately around 1% each, contributing to the strong emotional volatility of the market.

Dong Loc et al. (2010) reviewed developments in the Stock Trading Centre (STC) in Ho Chi Minh City, the precedent of the current HSX to test the weak-form efficiency of the Vietnamese stock market. An important element of the investigation concerns the possible bias of the results caused by the thin trading that characterizes the STC. The main conclusion of this paper is that the STC is not efficient in the weak form.

Phan and Zhou (2014) discussed the weak-form efficiency for the Vietnamese stock market. The paper tested the random walk hypothesis for weekly stock market returns employing the autocorrelation test, variance ratio test, and runs test for the period from July 2000 to July 2013. Results have strongly rejected the random walk hypothesis for the whole period and two out of the three cycles of the market. Interestingly, the third cycle alone (from February 2009 to July 2013) provided evidence supporting the random walk hypothesis in the stock index of HSX (VN-Index) showing that the efficiency of the Vietnamese stock market has gradually been improved during nearly 10 years in operation.

Cuong and Jian (2014) applied Theory of Planned Behavior (TPB) to explore the impact of factors influencing individuals' investment behavioral intention in the Vietnamese stock market. Results found in this research have supported the hypotheses that an individual investor's investment intention is significantly affected by three factors mentioned in the original TPB model including attitude, subjective norm and perceived behavioral control. The study also found evidence that psychological factors and also gender have a significant impact on the individuals' attitude towards investment.

Vo (2015) discussed the role of foreign investors in reducing market volatility using panel data analysis and found evidence supporting this hypothesis. A suggestion for a higher ratio of foreign investor existence was also proposed.

However, there was no paper mentioned AMH for the Vietnamese stock market in the literature the authors have researched, setting up a research gap for further evaluations and evidence of this market's efficiency. Also, in line with the assumption of the varying efficiency from time to time of the AMH, there were signals from the market movements showing that Vietnamese markets might have learned to adapt through time, and became more stable after each period of turmoil, and a test for AMH in the Vietnamese market context shall contribute to answering the question of efficiency.

2. Methods and Data Sources

2.1. Methods

This paper examines the AMH theory in two ways: a battery of autocorrelation tests and a time-varying autoregressive model.

The first battery of tests includes popular serial correlation tests, i.e., the automatic variance ratio (AVR) test, automatic portmanteau (AO) test, the generalized spectral (GS) test. These tests detect the linear and non-linear relationships in a time series, from which a conclusion regarding the validation of the AMH theory can be made.

The second method is involved with the construction of a time-varying autoregressive ("TV-AR") model, i.e., an autoregressive model with the coefficients changing over time. This is a fairly new testing method, which has been introduced in the work of Ito et al. (2014). This method possesses several advantages over other testing methods.

The details of the methods are presented in the following sections.

2.1.1. Autocorrelation Testing Approach

This paper quantifies the market efficiency through three tests of autocorrelation to examine whether the level of market efficiency significantly changes over time, aiming at evaluating the weak-form efficiency of the stock market. The task usually requires autocorrelation tests. The common understanding is that if time series data exhibit significant autocorrelations, it will be easier to predict the stock returns using historical prices, and the investors will obtain abnormal gains more easily. In other words, the more serially correlated the time series data are, the lower the market efficiency is.

Among popular autocorrelation tests, the paper adopted the following quantitative tests:

- Automatic Variance Ratio ("AVR") test;
- Automatic Portmanteau ("AP") test; and
- Generalized Spectral ("GS") test

The main reason why these tests are utilized is that these tests work on data which suffer from conditional heteroskedasticity, which is a common symptom of financial time series. This is also the case of Vietnamese stock market indices—in fact, a simple plotting (i.e., Figures 1 and 2) shows that both VN-INDEX data and HNX-INDEX data exhibit the conditional heteroskedasticity:

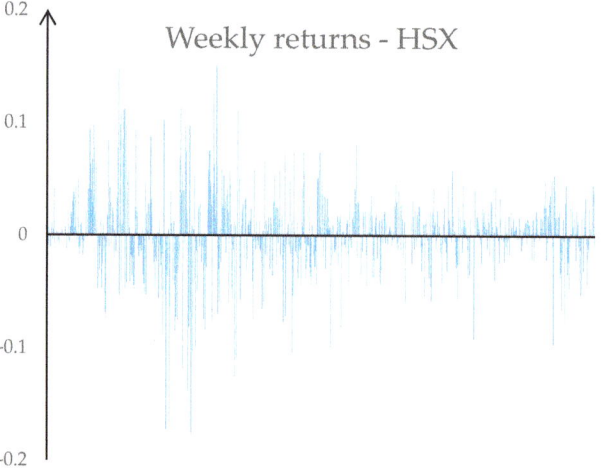

Figure 1. The weekly returns of HSX in the period from 2005 to 2019.

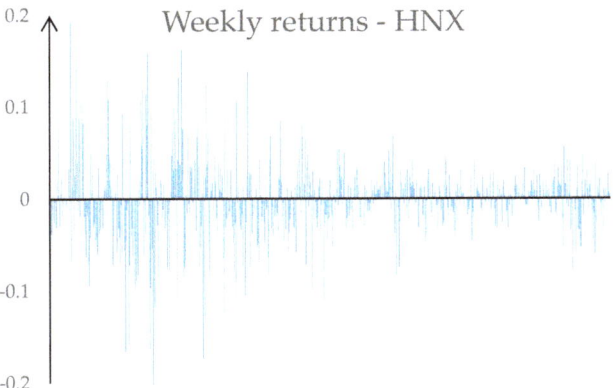

Figure 2. The weekly returns of Hanoi Stock Exchange (HNX) in the period from 2006 to 2019.

There is visual evidence of conditional heteroskedasticity in both plots above that the series of returns since volatility clustering can be observed. Particularly, the weeks with large variances in weekly returns cluster in the period from 2006 to 2010 and the weeks with smaller variance clusters in more recent periods. Due to such symptom, the paper opts to the three tests above to analyze this type of data. On a side note, the AVR test and the GS test employ the wild bootstrapping approach, which is most suited for data of small sample size like Vietnamese stock indices.

Each test possesses different statistical characteristics, which can be complementary to one another. The characteristics are as follows:

- The AVR test, which is modified from the traditional variance ratio test, is the most popular test in the AMH examination. This is the primary testing method of this paper.
- The AP test is an asymptotic test, which relies on the squared correlation coefficients. This method eliminates the possibility that the positive correlations and the negative correlations offset one another (Kim et al. 2011).
- The GS test is an autocorrelation test that can determine the non-linear relationship in the data series. The non-linear relationship in stock data can be recognized (Lim and Brooks 2011), yet cannot be detected by popular linear tests such as the AVR test and the AP test.

These tests are conducted with the *"vrtest"* package in R. Specifically, the test statistics were calculated on the basis of the rolling window method with a fixed 1-year window length. In fact, the window length observably had a minimal effect on the test results according to the work of Kim et al. (2011). Afterward, the quantitative results were assessed qualitatively to examine the impact of market conditions on the degree of market efficiency.

The details on how to conduct each test are as follows:

- The Automatic Variance Ratio (AVR) test

The AVR test is developed based on the traditional variance ratio test (Lo and MacKinlay 1988), which is the most popular test of the random walk theory, according to Hoque et al. (2007). The test is based on the statistical feature that the variance of *k*-periods stock returns equals to *k* times the variance of 1-period stock returns, provided that the stock returns series follows a random walk.

The variance ratio is defined to be the weighted sum of correlation coefficients in the stock returns series:

$$VR(k) = \frac{\sigma_k^2}{k\,\sigma^2} = 1 + 2\sum_{j=1}^{k-1}(1-\frac{j}{k})\rho_j,$$

in which: σ_k^2 is the variance of *k*-period stock returns, σ^2 is the variance of 1-period stock returns. ρ_j is the *j*-degree correlation coefficient. The closer to 1 the VR test statistics are, the better the data series follow a random walk. If the VR test statistics are greater than 1, a positive correlation is concluded, otherwise, if such statistics are less than 1, the series is undergoing a mean reversion. The VR test statistics are estimated as follows:

$$VR(k) = \frac{\sigma_k^2}{k\,\sigma^2} = 1 + 2\sum_{j=1}^{k-1}(1-\frac{j}{k})\hat{\rho}_j$$

in which $\hat{\rho}_j$ is an estimate of ρ_j.

One major setback of this approach is that the value of k is selected based on personal perceptions. In other words, the traditional variance ratio approach is subjective and may provide irreproducible results. Choi (1999) proposed the automatic variance ratio test, which employs the data-oriented method to determine the optimal ($\hat{k}$). In the AVR test, Choi assumed that the stock returns series is identical and independently distributed, and claimed that:

$$AVR(\hat{k}) = \frac{\sqrt{\frac{T}{k}}[VR(\hat{k})-1]}{\sqrt{2}} \xrightarrow{d} N(0,1)$$

However, if the data suffered from conditional heteroskedasticity, the test results may not be reliable, especially when the sample size is small. In particular, the construction of confidence intervals following $N(0,1)$ distribution may not reflect the level of uncertainty in the estimate of k. Accordingly, Kim (2006) proposed an alternative to the normal distribution approach—the wild bootstrapping approach. This approach is proved to be more suitable than the simple residual bootstrapping method in case the data exhibits heteroskedasticity.

- The Automatic Portmanteau (AP) test

The AP test is a popular tool to detect autocorrelations in time series data. However, one shortcoming of the traditional AP test is that when the time series data suffer from conditional heteroskedasticity, the test statistics may be inaccurate. Accordingly, Lobato et al. (2001) suggested an advanced AP test, which utilizes the following test statistics:

$$Q_p^* = T\sum_{i=1}^{p}\tilde{\rho}_i^2$$

in which: $\tilde{\rho}_i^2 = \hat{\gamma}_i^2/\tau_i^2$ ($\hat{\gamma}_i^2$ is the estimator for the autocovariance of the time series data of order i, and τ_i^2 represents the autocovariance of the squared stock returns. Similar to the selection of k in the traditional VR test, the advanced AP test also suffers from irreproducibility as the selection of lag p is based on personal judgements. In order to fix the problem, Escanciano and Lobato (2009) proposed an automatic data-driven approach which determines the optimal lag p. The test statistics, therefore, can be calculated as follows:

$$AQ \equiv Q_p^* = T\sum_{i=1}^{\tilde{p}}\tilde{\rho}_i^2$$

In which, $\tilde{p}$ is the optimal estimator of lag p, determined by Akaike information criterion (AIC) or Bayesian information criterion (BIC). The AP test statistics follow the Chi-squared distribution with one degree of freedom.

- The Generalized Spectral (GS) test

The nonlinear correlation, which is ignored in the linear correlation tests such as the AVR test and the AP test, has been commonly detected in the stock returns (Lim and Brooks 2011).

Accordingly, Escanciano and Velasco (2006) proposed the generalized spectral test, which can assess the nonlinear relationship in time series data. This is based on the knowledge that when the stock return follows a general martingale difference sequence, its normalized spectral density function is equal to one at all frequencies. The paper suggests that the test statistics are to be calculated as follows:

$$D_n^2 = \sum_{j=1}^{n-1}(n-j)\frac{1}{(j\pi)^2}\int_{\mathbb{R}}|\hat{\gamma}_j(x)|^2 W(dx)$$

The paper also involved the wild bootstrapping method, in which they obtained the *p*-value of the test. If the *p*-value corresponding with the test statistics is less than 5%, it can be concluded that the market is inefficient at that point in time.

2.1.2. The Time-Varying Autoregressive (TV-AR) Approach

The time-varying autoregressive model is developed from the simple autoregressive model.

The simple autoregressive model has long been used to assess the linear relationship in time series data. However, one major drawback of this model is that the coefficients are fixed, and therefore the simple model cannot handle the time series data with structural breaks, such as stock returns.

Ito et al. (2014) introduced the time-varying autoregressive model as a solution for the aforementioned drawback. The detail on how to employ the model in the AMH testing is presented below.

Firstly, the optimal lag order for each series is chosen using the BIC. The optimal lag orders for VN-INDEX and HNX-INDEX are 2 and 1 correspondingly. Subsequently, a regression following the TV-AR model is conducted, of which the theoretical framework is elaborated below.

The TV-AR model is presented in the form of an equation system as follows (with the assumption that parameter dynamics restrict the parameters):

$$x_t = \alpha_0 + \alpha_{1,t}x_{t-1} + \alpha_{2,t}x_{t-2} + \cdots + \alpha_{q,t}x_{t-q} + u_t \quad (1)$$

$$\alpha_{i,t} = \alpha_{i,t-1} + v_{i,t} (i = 1, 2, \cdots, q) \quad (2)$$

$$E(u_t) = E(u_t^2) = E(u_t u_{t-m}) = 0 \ \forall m$$

$$E(v_{i,t}) = E(v_{i,t}^2) = E(v_{i,t}v_{t-m}) = 0 \ \forall m$$

where x_t represents the stock return at time t, α_i is the time-varying coefficients, u_t and v_t are the residuals of the model. (1) and (2) form a system of simultaneous equations for the model.

Denotation of matrices are deployed as follows:

$$X_{t-1} = \begin{bmatrix} x_{t-1} \\ x_{t-2} \\ \vdots \\ x_{t-q} \end{bmatrix}; A_t = [\alpha_{1,t}\alpha_{2,t} \cdots \alpha_{q,t}]; I_q \text{ is an identity matrix of order } q.$$

Equation (1) can be rewritten accordingly:

$$x_t = \alpha_0 + X_{t-1}^T \times A_t^T + U_t$$

where X_{t-1}^T, A_t^T are the transpose of X_{t-1}, A_t correspondingly.

Assign a range of values (from 1 to T) to the parameter t to obtain the following equation:

$$\begin{bmatrix} x_1 \\ x_2 \\ \vdots \\ x_T \end{bmatrix} = \begin{bmatrix} 1 & X_0^T & & O_{1 \times T} \\ 1 & & X_1^T & \\ \vdots & & & \ddots \\ 1 & O_{1 \times T} & & X_{T-1}^T \end{bmatrix} \times \begin{bmatrix} \alpha_0 \\ A_1^T \\ \vdots \\ A_T^T \end{bmatrix} + \begin{bmatrix} u_1 \\ u_2 \\ \vdots \\ u_T \end{bmatrix} \quad (3)$$

$$\text{Denote} \, y = \begin{bmatrix} x_1 \\ x_2 \\ \vdots \\ x_T \end{bmatrix}; \, \beta = \begin{bmatrix} \alpha_0 \\ A_1^T \\ \vdots \\ A_T^T \end{bmatrix}; \, U = \begin{bmatrix} u_1 \\ u_2 \\ \vdots \\ u_T \end{bmatrix}; \, M = \begin{bmatrix} 1 & X_0^T & & O_{1 \times T} \\ 1 & & X_1^T & \\ \vdots & & & \ddots \\ 1 & O_{1 \times T} & & X_{T-1}^T \end{bmatrix}$$

where $O_{1 \times T}$ is a $1 \times T$ null matrix.

Equation (3) can be simplified accordingly:

$$y = M \times \beta + U \quad (4)$$

In a similar manner, Equation (2) can be re-written as:

$$\begin{bmatrix} -A_0^T \\ 0 \\ \vdots \\ 0 \end{bmatrix} = \begin{bmatrix} O_{q \times 1} & -I_q & & O_{q \times q} \\ O_{q \times 1} & I_q & -I_q & \\ \vdots & \vdots & & \ddots \\ O_{q \times 1} & O_{q \times q} & \cdots & -I_q \end{bmatrix} \times \begin{bmatrix} \alpha_0 \\ A_1^T \\ \vdots \\ A_T^T \end{bmatrix} + \begin{bmatrix} v_1 \\ v_2 \\ \vdots \\ v_T \end{bmatrix}$$

$$\text{Denote:} \, Z = \begin{bmatrix} -A_0^T \\ 0 \\ \vdots \\ 0 \end{bmatrix}; \, W = \begin{bmatrix} O_{q \times 1} & -I_q & & O_{q \times q} \\ O_{q \times 1} & I_q & -I_q & \\ \vdots & \vdots & & \ddots \\ O_{q \times 1} & O_{q \times q} & \cdots & -I_q \end{bmatrix}; \, V = \begin{bmatrix} v_1 \\ v_2 \\ \vdots \\ v_T \end{bmatrix}$$

The following equation is obtained:

$$z = W \times \beta + V \quad (5)$$

Equations (4) and (5) form the equation system of the TV-AR model in the matrix form. It can also be further deducted as below:

$$\begin{bmatrix} y \\ z \end{bmatrix} = \begin{bmatrix} M \\ W \end{bmatrix} \beta + \begin{bmatrix} U \\ V \end{bmatrix}$$

The result below is obtained using ordinary least squares (OLS) regression:

$$\hat{\beta} = \left(\begin{bmatrix} M \\ W \end{bmatrix}^T \begin{bmatrix} M \\ W \end{bmatrix} \right)^{-1} \begin{bmatrix} M \\ W \end{bmatrix}^T \begin{bmatrix} y \\ z \end{bmatrix}$$

The market efficiency is quantified using the following formula, which was used in the work of Noda (2016), a special case of Ito et al. (2014):

$$\text{MEt} = \left| \frac{\sum_{j=1}^{p} \hat{\alpha}_{j,t}}{1 - \left(\sum_{j=1}^{p} \hat{\alpha}_{j,t} \right)} \right|$$

This formula measures the deviation from the zero coefficients of the corresponding time-varying moving average (TV-MA) model to our TV-AR model. Hence, the large deviations of MEt from zero is considered evidence of market inefficiency.

Lastly, the authors also employ the bootstrap procedure to construct the confidence band for ME_t. The detail of the bootstrapping steps is elaborated in the work of Noda (2016). The bootstrap is conducted under the null hypothesis of zero autocorrelations with 2000 iterations.

2.2. Data

The primary data used in this paper are the weekly stock returns in HNX and HSX, calculated based on the HNX-INDEX and VN-INDEX correspondingly as below:

$$r_t = \ln\left(\frac{P_t}{P_{t-1}}\right) = \ln(P_t) - \ln(P_{t-1})$$

where:

r_t is the weekly stock returns at week t
P_t is the value of VN-INDEX/HNX-INDEX at the last trading day of week t
P_{t-1} is the value of VN-INDEX/HNX-INDEX at the last trading day of week $(t-1)$

VN-INDEX data are collected from January 2005 to February 2019, which skipped the first 5 years from 2000 to 2004 of HSX due to the lack of trading activities during this period. HNX-INDEX is collected from May 2006 to February 2019. The data were collected from the online portals of two Vietnamese securities companies, namely VNDIRECT Securities Company and Bao Viet Securities Company (Supplementary Materials).

3. Empirical Results and Discussion

3.1. AVR Test Results

Figure 3 presents the AVR test results at HSX. The red line represents the AVR test statistics, while the dotted black line represents the upper bound and lower bound of the confidence interval.

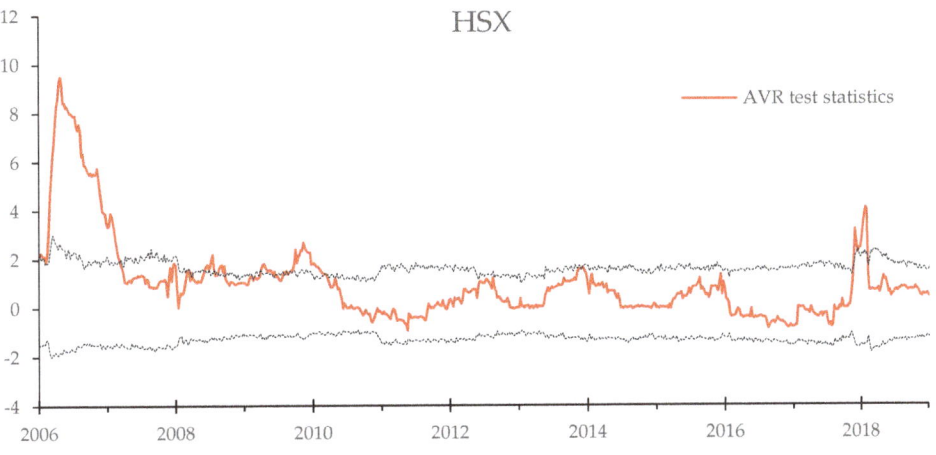

Figure 3. Automatic variance ratio (AVR) test results for HSX.

In general, HSX stock prices were unstable in the first post-creation years, but recently, such variations have been lessened. The market efficiency has improved significantly.

The period from 2006 to 2008 witnessed the peak of AVR statistics, which marked the most inefficient period of HSX. It is worth noting that, during this period, Vietnam was severely impacted by the global financial crisis, with VN-INDEX dropped from more than 70% in just one year. Investors heavily relied on the majority to make trading decisions instead of on the available market information. Not until 2008 did the AVR test statistics drop to the normal level (i.e., within the confidence interval), meaning the market achieved efficiency. This behavior is in line with Kim et al.'s (2011) finding that market efficiency hit bottom in the event of a market crisis and reached its peak when the market crashed.

During the 2008–2010 period, the AVR test statistics were generally greater than the upper bound but not by a large amount. This implies that the market retrieved its stability, but was still considered inefficient, which is likely due to the lasting effect of the financial crisis.

In the first few months of 2011, the AVR statistics continued to drop to nearly zero. This happened at the same time with the global financial crisis, which resulted from the government debt crisis in Greece. This behavior, once again, validates the finding of Kim et al. (2011). More importantly, the impact of the succeeding crisis was not as strong as the preceding one, most probably because investors were becoming better informed and cautious in trading activities. In fact, the herd mentality in 2011 was much less serious in 2007, as the market capitalization only increased by 140% in 2010 in comparison with an increase of 1100% in 2006. This further proves the adaptive nature of the market, which is also an important implication of the AMH theory.

From 2012 until recently, the AVR statistics have stayed within the confidence interval most of the time. The AVR statistics occasionally crossed the upper bound and went up (at the beginning of 2018, with an expectation of increasing risk level due to the worsening U.S-China trade war, interest hike and quantitative tightening), nevertheless, the test statistics have never been too far off the band and quickly reverted in a short period of time. It can be concluded that while HSX may not be fully efficient, it has improved substantially in such regard.

The AVR test statistics of HNX are demonstrated in Figure 4 below:

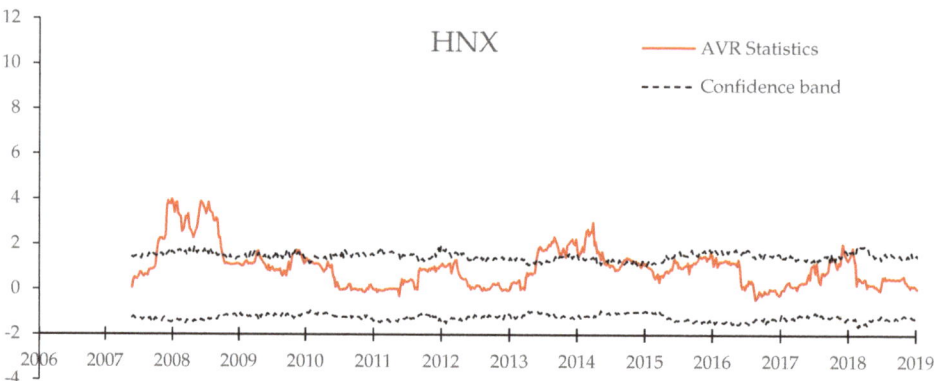

Figure 4. AVR test results in HNX.

In the first post-creation years, the AVR test statistics at HNX had been remarkably high, which is likely to result from the market inefficiency and the negative effect of the financial crisis in 2007 and 2011. From 2011 onwards, the AVR test statistics in HNX gained stability and have been highly correlated with the test statistics in HSX. This suggests that the market efficiency of HNX, despite the market's most recent formation, has experienced periods of efficiency and inefficiency although it has been dependent on market conditions.

In conclusion, according to the AVR test statistics, the market efficiency in both exchanges expressed the same behavior: It has been varying over time, with alternating periods of efficiency and periods of inefficiency. In addition, the study proves that market efficiency is affected by market conditions.

3.2. AP Test Results

The purpose of the AP test is to solidify the AVR test results and to make sure that no positive and negative correlations are canceled out. The AP test results of HSX and HNX are illustrated in Figures 5 and 6 correspondingly, with the red line representing the test statistics and the black dotted line representing the F-statistics at 5% significance level:

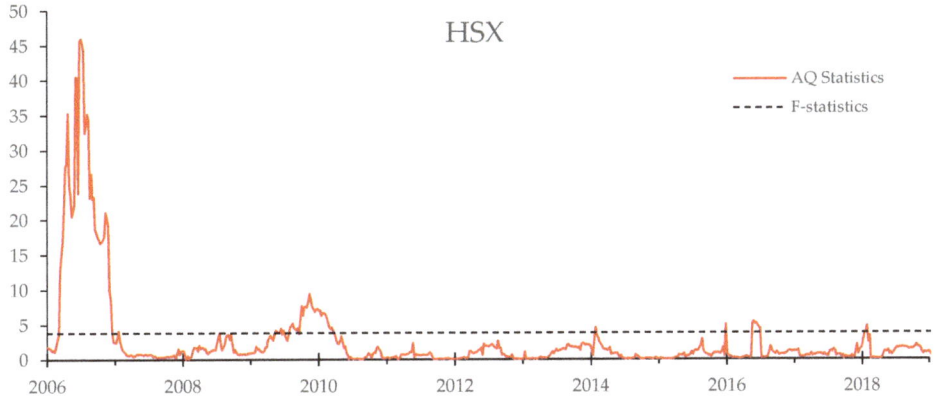

Figure 5. The Automatic Portmanteau (AP) results of HSX.

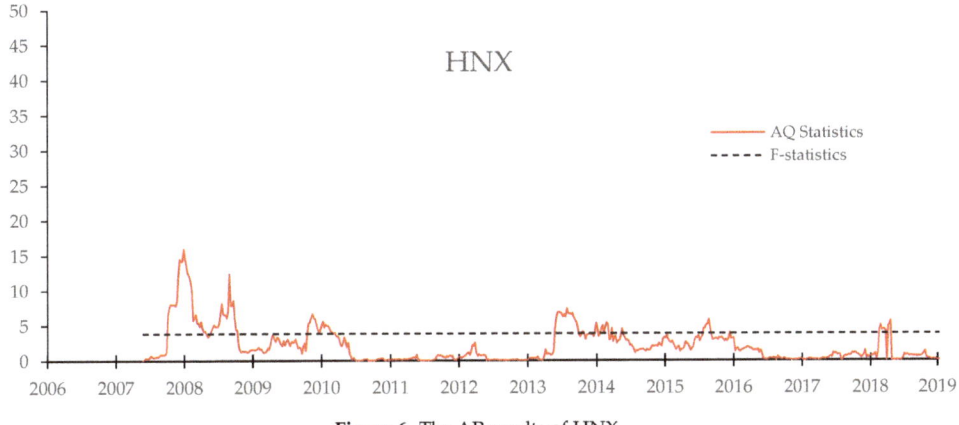

Figure 6. The AP results of HNX.

The results are highly consistent with the AVR test results, which implies that no correlations with the opposites canceled out each other. The AP results also confirm the AMH theory in the case of the Vietnamese stock market.

3.3. The GS Test Statistics

The GS test statistics are utilized to detect the non-linear relationship within time series data. The *p*-values of GS test results of HSX and HNX are presented in Figures 7 and 8, with the red line being the *p*-values and the black dotted line being the 5% significance level.

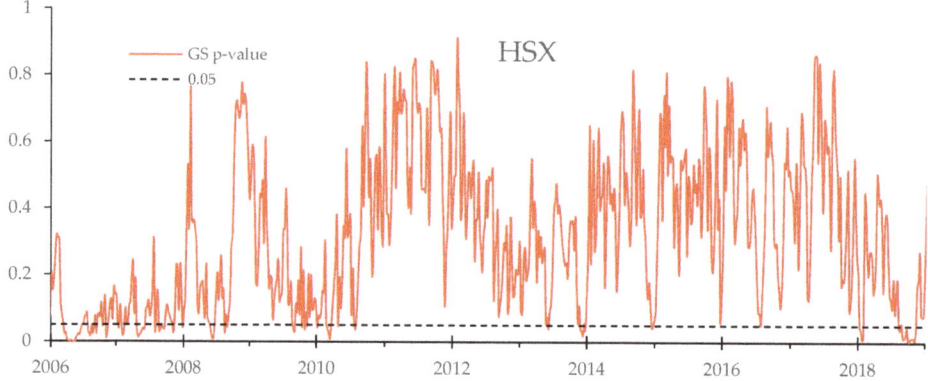

Figure 7. The generalized spectral (GS) results of HSX.

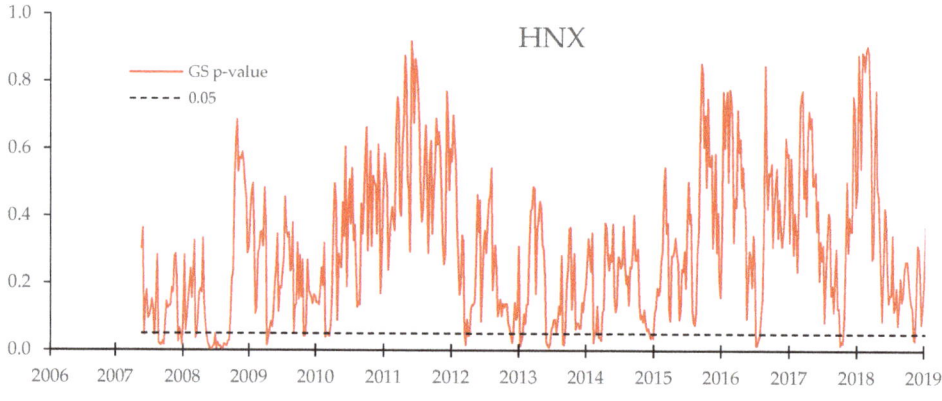

Figure 8. Results of HNX.

The *p*-values of the GS test results indicate that market efficiency has undergone many alternating periods of efficiency and inefficiency. The test also reveals a few periods of inefficiency that were omitted in the previous two tests, implying the existence of significant non-linear autocorrelations in stock prices.

The line representing the GS test *p*-value might look different from the line representing the AVR test statistics and the AP test statistics. This is mainly due to the fact that market efficiency is indicated by lower test statistics in the AVR test and AP test; meanwhile, it is indicated by a higher p-value in the GS test. Therefore, the GS test resultsis still considered to be highly consistent with the previous tests, which confirm the AMH theory in the Vietnamese stock market.

3.4. The TV-AR Approach

The degree of market efficiency ME_t obtained from this approach is presented in Figures 9 and 10, with the red line being the value of ME_t and the black dotted line being the 5% significance level.

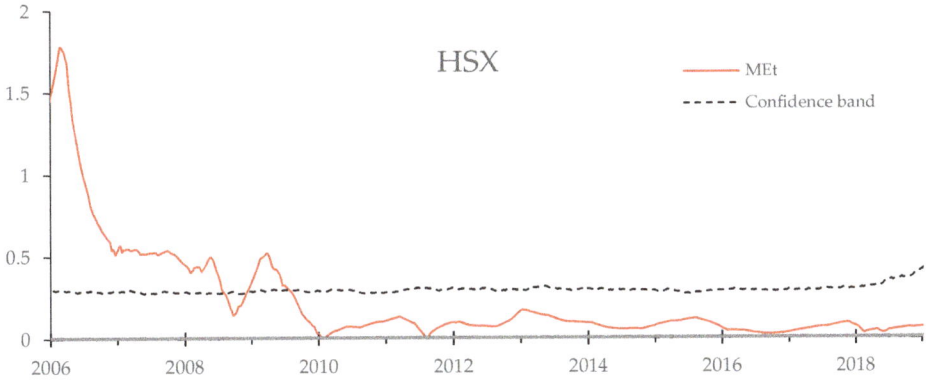

Figure 9. The time-varying autoregressive (TV-AR) result in HSX.

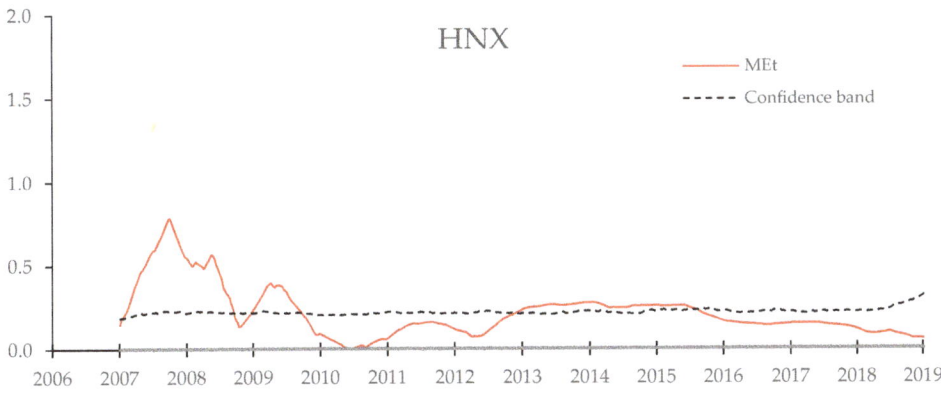

Figure 10. The TV-AR result of HNX.

It can be observed that the results of the TV-AR are highly consistent with the other battery of autocorrelation tests. This serves as a validation for the battery of autocorrelation tests, that the results of the autocorrelation tests are robust and the conclusions remain consistent with a different approach.

4. Limitations and Suggestions

The most significant drawback of this research paper is that the second criterion proposed by Lim and Brooks (2011), i.e., the market efficiency should be dependent on market conditions, was only assessed qualitatively. This qualitative approach was selected due to the fact that the Vietnamese market had only undergone one brief period of stock market bubble-induced crisis, and therefore it impossible to form a large enough sample for a statistically meaningful analysis. Our future research will expand to cover further analysis using Bayesian network modeling with the R package Bayes VL (Vuong and La 2019) As a qualitative assessment might suffer from the subjective opinion of the authors, the paper cannot provide a strong argument for that matter.

Our recommended workaround for this drawback is to pool a large sample of stock indices, including the Vietnamese stock indices and other comparable indices from other countries which are similar to Vietnam. The data should be collected in the form of panel data, so the data in relation to market conditions can be large enough to provide a correct inference. This approach requires that researchers have the sound knowledge of the Vietnamese stock market and the stock markets in similar countries, and that the selected approach should be compatible with panel data.

5. Conclusions

This paper aims to examine the AMH theory in the Vietnamese stock market through a battery of autocorrelation tests, namely the AVR test, the AP test, and the GS test, and a time-varying autoregressive approach. The rolling window method is used with the fixed 2-year window length.

The AVR test, the primary testing method of this paper results in different times of efficiency and inefficiency, with the strongest AVR statistics in the crisis period 2007–2008 in Vietnam. There were consequent signals of inefficiency afterward, but the level was decreasing over time, consistent with the AMH. Test results are in general identical between HSX and HNX.

In order to eliminate the effect of signs, the AP test which relies on the squared correlation coefficients is employed. The outcome of AP test shows consistency with the AVR test, rejecting the effect of signs offsetting.

The non-linear relationship which cannot be detected by linear tests is examined by the GS test, and despite having similar results to the aforementioned tests, it does show some inefficiencies which are missed by linear testing methods.

Aside from the battery of statistical tests, we have also fitted a TV-AR model, which serves as an alternative approach and a robustness check for the testing results. In the TV-AR model, the deviation of coefficients is the proxy for the degree of market inefficiency. Accordingly, we have found that the result of the TV-AR approach is highly consistent with the result of the other approach. The result shows that the market inefficiency peaked and dropped in the period 2006–2008 and 2011, similar to the findings in the battery of autocorrelation tests.

The main implications of the tests are summarized below:

Evidence of market inefficiency is significant in financial crises, i.e., the period 2006–2007 and 2011, followed by a normalization phase when the market crashed and market efficiency was back to normal. This behavior is found to be consistent with those in the study conducted by Kim et al. (2011), which discovered that the market efficiency slumped in the event of financial crises and peaked when the market crashed.

Moreover, we also found that the impact of the financial crisis in 2011 was less severe than that of the financial crisis in 2007, which is likely due to an increase in investors' rationality. In other words, there is evidence suggesting that market behaviors have gradually improved—which is a critical implication of AMH theory.

In conclusion, as the Vietnamese stock market efficiency are both varying over time and influenced by the market conditions, it is concluded that the behavior of the Vietnamese stock market is in line with the adaptive market hypothesis.

Supplementary Materials: The following are available online at http://www.mdpi.com/1911-8074/12/2/81/s1.

Author Contributions: Both the authors were involved in conceptualization and writing. D.P.T.T. provided contributions to concept development, statistical model checks and results discussion. H.P.Q. provided contributions to methodology and data analysis, and R software analysis deployment.

Funding: This paper is funded by Research Project coded B2019-NTH-02 from Ministry of Education and Training, Vietnam.

Conflicts of Interest: The authors declare no conflict of interest.

References

Choi, In. 1999. Testing the Random Walk Hypothesis for Real Exchange Rates. *Journal of Applied Econometrics* 14: 293–308. [CrossRef]

Cuong, Phan Khoa, and Zhou Jian. 2014. Factors influencing individual investors' behavior: An empirical study of the Vietnamese stock market. *American Journal of Business and Management* 3: 77–94. [CrossRef]

Dong Loc, Truong, Ger Lanjouw, and Robert Lensink. 2010. Stock-market efficiency in thin-trading markets: The case of the Vietnamese stock market. *Applied Economics* 42: 3519–32. [CrossRef]

Escanciano, J. Carlos, and Carlos Velasco. 2006. Generalized Spectral Tests for the Martingale Difference Hypothesis. *Journal of Econometrics* 134: 151–85. [CrossRef]

Escanciano, J. Carlos, and Ignacio N. Lobato. 2009. Testing the Martingale Hypothesis. *Palgrave Handbook of Econometrics*, 972–1003.

Fama, Eugene F. 1970. Efficient Capital Markets: A Review of Theory and Empirical Work. *The Journal of Finance* 25: 383–417. [CrossRef]

Hiremath, Gourishankar S., and Jyoti Kumari. 2014. Stock Returns Predictability and the Adaptive Market Hypothesis in Emerging Markets: Evidence from India. *SpringerPlus* 3: 428. [CrossRef]

Hoque, Hafiz A.A.B., Jae H. Kim, and Chong Soo Pyun. 2007. A Comparison of Variance Ratio Tests of Random Walk: A Case of Asian Emerging Stock Markets. *International Review of Economics & Finance* 16: 488–502.

Ito, Mikio, Akihiko Noda, and Tatsuma Wada. 2014. International Stock Market Efficiency: A Non-Bayesian Time-Varying Model Approach. *Applied Economics* 46: 2744–54. [CrossRef]

Ito, Mikio, and Shunsuke Sugiyama. 2009. Measuring the Degree of Time Varying Market Inefficiency. *Economics Letters* 103: 62–64. [CrossRef]

Ito, Mikio, Akihiko Noda, and Tatsuma Wada. 2016. The evolution of stock market efficiency in the US: A non-Bayesian time-varying model approach. *Applied Economics* 48: 621–35. [CrossRef]

Kim, Jae H. 2006. Wild Bootstrapping Variance Ratio Tests. *Economics Letters* 92: 38–43. [CrossRef]

Kim, Jae H., Abul Shamsuddin, and Kian-Ping Lim. 2011. Stock Return Predictability and the Adaptive Markets Hypothesis: Evidence from Century-Long U.S. Data. *Journal of Empirical Finance* 18: 868–79. [CrossRef]

Lim, Kian-Ping, and Robert Brooks. 2011. The evolution of stock market efficiency over time: A survey of the empirical literature. *Journal of Economic Surveys* 25: 69–108. [CrossRef]

Lim, Kian-Ping, Robert Darren Brooks, and Melvin Hinich. 2006. Testing the Assertion That Emerging Asian Stock Markets Are Becoming More Efficient. *SSRN Journal*. Available online: https://papers.ssrn.com/sol3/papers.cfm?abstract_id=906515 (accessed on 29 March 2019). [CrossRef]

Lim, Kian-Ping, Weiwei Luo, and Jae H. Kim. 2013. Are US Stock Index Returns Predictable? Evidence from Automatic Autocorrelation-Based Tests. *Applied Economics* 45: 953–62. [CrossRef]

Lo, Andrew W. 2004. The Adaptive Markets Hypothesis: Market Efficiency from an Evolutionary Perspective. *Journal of Portfolio Management* 30: 15–29. [CrossRef]

Lo, Andrew W. 2005. Reconciling Efficient Markets with Behavioral Finance: The Adaptive Markets Hypothesis. *Journal of Investment Consulting* 7: 21–44.

Lo, Andrew, and A. Craig MacKinlay. 1988. Stock Market Prices Do Not Follow Random Walks: Evidence From a Simple Specification Test. *Review of Financial Studies* 1: 41–66. [CrossRef]

Lobato, Ignacio, John C. Nankervis, and N. E. Savin. 2001. Testing for Autocorrelation Using a Modified Box-Pierce Q Test. *International Economic Review* 42: 187–205. [CrossRef]

Neely, Christopher J., Paul A. Weller, and Joshua M. Ulrich. 2009. The adaptive markets hypothesis: evidence from the foreign exchange market. *Journal of Financial and Quantitative Analysis* 44: 467–88. [CrossRef]

Noda, Akihiko. 2016. A Test of the Adaptive Market Hypothesis Using a Time-Varying AR Model in Japan. *Finance Research Letters* 17: 66–71. [CrossRef]

Phan, Khoa Cuong, and Jian Zhou. 2014. Market efficiency in emerging stock markets: A case study of the Vietnamese stock market. *IOSR Journal of Business and Management* 16: 61–73. [CrossRef]

Smith, Graham. 2012. The Changing and Relative Efficiency of European Emerging Stock Markets. *The European Journal of Finance* 18: 689–708. [CrossRef]

Urquhart, Andrew, and Frank McGroarty. 2014. Calendar effects, market conditions and the Adaptive Market Hypothesis: Evidence from long-run US data. *International Review of Financial Analysis* 35: 154–66. [CrossRef]

Vo, Xuan Vinh. 2015. Foreign ownership and stock return volatility–Evidence from Vietnam. *Journal of Multinational Financial Management* 30: 101–9. [CrossRef]

Vu, Thi Hanh, Nguyen Van Duy, Ho Manh Tung, and Vuong Quan Hoang. 2019. Determinants of Vietnamese Listed firms performance: Competition, Wage, CEO, Firm Size, Age, and International Trade. *Journal of Risk and Financial Management* 12: 62. [CrossRef]

Vuong, Quan Hoang, and Viet Phuong La. 2019. BayesVL Package for Bayesian Statistical Analyses in R. Github: BayesVL version 0.6.5. Available online: https://github.com/sshpa/bayesvl (accessed on 7 May 2019). [CrossRef]

Vuong, Quan Hoang. 2018. The Financial Economy of Viet Nam in an Age of Reform, 1986–2016. Routledge Handbook of Banking and Finance in Asia Routledge. Available online: http://www.routledgehandbooks.com/doi/10.4324/9781315543222-12 (accessed on 7 May 2019).

Vuong, Quan-Hoang. 2019. Computational entrepreneurship: From Economic Complexities to Interdisciplinary. *Problems and Perspective in Management* 17: 117–29. [CrossRef]

© 2019 by the authors. Licensee MDPI, Basel, Switzerland. This article is an open access article distributed under the terms and conditions of the Creative Commons Attribution (CC BY) license (http://creativecommons.org/licenses/by/4.0/).

Journal of
Risk and Financial Management

Article

Determinants of Vietnamese Listed Firm Performance: Competition, Wage, CEO, Firm Size, Age, and International Trade

Thi-Hanh Vu [1], Van-Duy Nguyen [2], Manh-Tung Ho [3,4] and Quan-Hoang Vuong [3,4,*]

1. School of Economics and International Business, Foreign Trade University, 91 Chua Lang Street, Dong Da District, Hanoi 100000, Vietnam; hanhvt@ftu.edu.vn
2. Quantitative Analysis Center, QA Global Co., 9/82 Chua Lang street, Dong Da District, Hanoi 100000, Vietnam; duynguyen.qa@gmail.com
3. Center for Interdisciplinary Social Research, Phenikaa University, Yen Nghia, Ha Dong District, Hanoi 100803, Vietnam; tung.homanh@phenikaa-uni.edu.vn
4. Faculty of Economics and Finance, Phenikaa University, Yen Nghia, Ha Dong District, Hanoi 100803, Vietnam
* Correspondence: hoang.vuongquan@phenikaa-uni.edu.vn

Received: 17 March 2019; Accepted: 9 April 2019; Published: 11 April 2019

Abstract: This study investigates the relationship between firms' competition, wage, CEOs' characteristics, and firm performance (measured by net income per employee, return on assets (ROA) and return on equity (ROE)) of Vietnam's 693 listed firms in 2015 using both the ordinary-least-square (OLS) and quantile regression methods. Triangulating the results coming from the analysis of three different measures of firm performance, this study consistently confirms that the sex of CEOs and chairman turns out to be insignificant in explaining firm performance and there is a negative association between capital intensity and firm performance. For financial firms, the age of a firm and average wage per employee are negatively associated with all types of firm performance. The quantile regression method shows that the age of a firm is negatively correlated with its net income per employee for small firms, while it is insignificant for medium-sized firms. Meanwhile, firm size is positively associated with firm performance. These results indicate Vietnam's business activities are still concentrating on low labor cost, labor intensive, and low-tech production, thus, policies that promote innovation and high-tech applications should be encouraged.

Keywords: competition; wage; net income per employee; firm performance; productivity; Vietnam; listed company

1. Introduction

In the age of rapid digitization and globalization, companies worldwide are facing increasing pressure to innovate, increase productivity, and increase competitiveness. While this emerging trend is clearer than ever when looking at the rise of "computational entrepreneurship" in developed countries, what remains elusive is whether this is the case in developing countries (Vuong 2019a). In order to foster a more technologically advanced entrepreneurship, it is first and foremost necessary to go back to the micro level and examine the factors that affect firm performance, whether high- or low-tech. Understanding firm performance requires a thorough grasp of a firm's characteristics and its entrepreneurial endeavors. The current research looks at the transitional economy of Vietnam whose emerging market characteristics have captured the interests of academics over the past decades. Through an investigation of the performance of nearly 700 listed companies on Vietnam's stock markets, this study will triangulate the empirical results of three different indicators of a firm's performance: net income per employee, return on assets (ROA), and return on equity (ROE). It is hoped that robust evidence on the correlates of firm performance can be found. As such, the current study not only adds to the related literature on the issue, but also highlights, once again, a gap in the application of technology among public companies in Vietnam. The next subsections will review the relevant studies that have been done all over the world and in Vietnam to call attention to the scanty empirical evidence coming from the emerging market of nearly 100 million people with the Gross Domestic Products (GDP) at USD 204 billion in 2015 and a growth rate over 6% since then (Vuong 2019b).

1.1. Studies on the Correlates of Firm Performance around the World

Given the importance of explaining firm performance, a large volume of research in this area has focused on uncovering various factors associated with firm performance. Considering the effect of female leadership, there is more evidence for the positive impact of having a female in the top position of a company on their performance. Dezsö and Ross (2012) analyzed 15 years of panel data from the S&P 1500 firm and found having a female in top management does improve firm performance, given that innovation is the focus of a firm's strategy. Dezsö and Ross used Tobin's Q as the primary measure of firm performance. In a similar vein, Lückerath-Rovers (2013) found that companies with women on board are performing better than those without through analyzing 99 listed firms in the Dutch Female Board Index. Using different measures of performance, such as return on assets (ROA), other studies found a positive correlation between having female in the board of directors and performance (Carter et al. 2003; Krishnan and Park 2005). In contrast, in a Danish study, Rose (2007) did not find any significant relationship. This inconsistency might be explained by the sampling methods or cultural factors or even study designs. In many cases, it is a not a straightforward link between having women directors and better performance. For example, a study in China investigated this question among China's listed firms from 1999 to 2011 and found the type of ownership can be a mitigating factor: state-controlled firms are less likely to benefit from having female leaders (Liu et al. 2014).

Regarding competition as a correlate of firm performance, Schiffbauer and Ospina (2006) attempted to measure a firm's productivity in four different ways, among which the total factor productivity (TFP) is employed under an augmented Cobb–Douglas production function. They found that in countries that reformed during 2004, firms experienced a more pronounced increase in competition and in turn, productivity. Pressure from international competition can also exert positive influence, greater international competition enlarges the relevant market and can affect both the number and the type of competitors a firm faces (De Loecker and Biesebroeck 2018). Regarding competition effects across product markets, high rent firms (firms that are able to earn profits beyond a competitive level) had consistently lower productivity growth than low rent firms (Nickell 1996). More recently, Bourlès et al. (2013) considered the impact of competition in intermediate goods markets on downstream productivity. Notably, their evidence shows that anticompetitive upstream regulations have significantly curbed TFP growth, particularly for firms that are close to the productivity frontier.

In 2012, Wager surveyed the literature on international trade and firm performance attempting to establish the links between exports and imports activities and various dimensions of firm performance (productivity, wages, profitability, and survival). Wagner found that a large amount of empirical studies in various countries points to the same direction: international training firms perform better in terms of productivity than nonexporters and nonimporters. However, this trend must be interpreted with caution due to the absence of comparable sample size (Wagner 2012). Andersson et al. (2012) presented an analysis of international trade engagement of Swedish firms, showing the relationship between firm performance and international trade is not straightforwardly about a firm being an exporter or nonexporter; the geographical nature of export and import activities also has a statistically significant effect on firm's productivity. In a study on Portuguese manufacturing firms, two-ways traders are shown to perform better than only exporters or only importers. Moreover, intensity of international training activities, diversity of market goods, and destination of products are also explanatory for better performance (Silva et al. 2013). A study in 2018 suggests the gain in firm performance is three times higher than the direct costs of export promotion (Munch and Schaur 2018).

Considering the relationship of wage and firm performance, an empirical study using a dataset of 200,000 French firms between 1995 to 2007 found that firm size regulation seems to result in a loss in productivity as many productive firms choose to stay below the threshold of firm size to avoid regulation. These productive firms are allocated too little employment and must bear implicit labor tax; the reducing equilibrium wages encourages more people who work as small entrepreneurs rather than working as employees for more productive firms (Garicano et al. 2016). Regarding firm size, empirical studies on corporate finance have commonly used firm size as an important and a fundamental firm characteristic. This factor is worth considering given that business regulations or taxation policies often differ among big, medium, and small firms, which would in turn affect the firm's performance (Garicano et al. 2016, 2017). Additionally, firm size is empirically found to have positive association with capital structure, such that bigger firms may have higher leverage in external financing (Kurshev and Strebulaev 2015). On the relationship between firm size and firm performance, studies have sought to compare the level of competitiveness or corporate social performance between small and big firms. For instance, Wolff and Pett (2000) noted that when it comes to the internationalization of small U.S. firms, the larger ones did show competitive patterns consistent with their size-related resource base, as opposed to the smaller ones. Meanwhile, scholars have confirmed the positive correlation of corporate social performance and financial performance in firms with a large size (Orlitzky 2001; Schreck and Raithel 2015). In terms of sustainability performance, small and medium enterprises, particularly in the food supply chain, are found to be more susceptible to high social, environmental, and economic pressures than larger enterprises. In one study in Turkey, the researchers found a positive correlation between the size indicators of a firm and its performance (Doğan 2013).

Researchers have also tried to uncover other factors that can influence firm performance. Sun and Yu (2015), for example, found a positive correlation between performance (measured by sales per employees and net income per employee) and Corporate Social Responsibility (CSR) practices and firms without. Choudhary (2014) looked at the impact of smartphones use on net income per employee and found they have a positive correlation. Camisón and Villar-López (2014) analyzed a dataset of 144 Spanish firms and found that organizational innovation does have a positive effect on technological capabilities, which in turn tends to cause better firm performance. A study on 89 high-tech firms in Jiangsu province, China revealed that knowledge sharing, whether explicit or implicit, does support innovation and performance (Wang and Wang 2012). A study in Tunisia looked at the relationship between information and communication technologies (ICTs) use and the performance of Tunisian SMEs (measured by net profit margins) and showed there is a significant association between the level of ICT use and firm performance (Piget and Kossaï 2013). The research area where correlates of firm performance are studied does fall into the larger context of understanding corporate governance. Interesting studies have been carried out, for example, on market competition (Giroud and Mueller 2011), CEO tournament as governance (Coles et al. 2017), compensation incentives (Core and Guay 1999), or mutual monitoring of executives (Li 2014) as governance mechanisms.

As shown above, although the literature on firm performance around the world is truly diverse, the same cannot be said about business research in Vietnam, an emerging economy which has only entered the lower middle income rank recently (Vuong 2019b). The next section will cover the meager ground of research on firm performance in Vietnam.

1.2. Studies on Firm Performance in Vietnam

In the recent years, Vietnam's now nearly 100 million people has been enjoying continuous economic growth for over 30 years, in this success, entrepreneurship and internationalization of the economy have played a crucial role. The state-led economic reform in 1896 has brought radical changes to the country; the country's GDP per capita has reached to nearly US$2300 in 2015 from only US$217 in 1989 (Vuong 2019b). It is estimated that in just 8 years from 1991 to 1999, there were around 40,000 newly established companies (Pham and Vuong 2009). Following this first generation of business ventures, the number of small and medium sized enterprises (SMEs) continued to increase from 349,000 in 2009 (Vuong and Tran 2009) to around 500,000 in 2017 (Nhan Dan 2017). In 2015, Vietnam was considered one of the most globalized populous economies in the world (Kopf 2018).

Recently, the arrival of Industry 4.0 has marked a new era for entrepreneurship in Vietnam (Vuong et al. 2019), the next generation of business ventures is now operating ever more on complex computational platforms, marking a shift to a new form of entrepreneurship: computational entrepreneurship (Vuong 2019a). In 2017, it is reported that Vietnam is among the countries with the highest total early-stage entrepreneurial activity—23.3%—and a significant entrepreneurial spirit index—0.26 (GERA 2018). Some of the successful startups are digital, such as Foody—a food delivery app, or Tiki—an e-commerce website, or WeFit—a fitness app allowing users to use gyms around a city.

Given the importance of successful entrepreneurship for Vietnam, it goes without saying understanding which factors influence firm performance is crucial. However, research in this area remains meager and scattered over the years, especially when it comes to listed companies. A comparative study between Thai and Vietnamese SMEs in 2003, found the difference in entrepreneurial orientation between Thai and Vietnamese business owners lead to difference in firm performance. Thai SMEs are more innovative and proactive, while Vietnamese SMEs are likely to take risks. Thai SMEs have higher perceived business growth, job creation, and net profit than Vietnamese SMEs (Swierczek and Ha 2003). Another study examined the impact of privatization by comparing the pre- and postprivatization financial and operating performance of 121 former state-owned enterprises (SOEs) (Truong et al. 2006). The results highlighted significant hikes in profitability, revenues, efficiency and employee income, in addition to confirming the key determinants of better performance to be firm size, residual state ownership, corporate governance, and stock listing (Truong et al. 2006).

More recent studies also noted that when ownership is concentrated, firms with residual state ownership see poorer performance than those with foreign ownership (Phung and Hoang 2013; Phung and Mishra 2016; Tran et al. 2014). These findings, however, are contested as another research that used data of listed firms in Vietnam reached the opposite conclusion—that foreign ownership turns out to have a negative impact on firm performance but positive impact on capital structure (Phung and Le 2013). Moreover, in a resource-constrained setting such as Vietnam, Vuong (2016a) shed light on the significant relationships between operational scales, financial resources and firms' performance, all the while highlighting the importance of an innovation strategy, as opposed to factors such as firm size, sales, and growth rate to Return-on-equity (ROE).

In a different approach on evaluating firm performance, Vo and Nguyen (2014) looked at a set of variables related to corporate governance. Particularly, upon analyzing a dataset of 177 listed Vietnamese companies from 2008–2012, the authors found that duality role of CEO and board independenance are positively correlated with firm performance. However, there was no empirical support for a relationship between board size and firm performance (Vo and Nguyen 2014). Additional studies have even noted a positive association between a firm's long-term credit financing relationship with banks and firm performance (Thanh and Ha 2013), a significantly negative relation between firm's debt ratio and its performance (Le and Phan 2017), a positive correlation between corporate social responsibility disclosures and firm value (Nguyen et al. 2015), and a significant and positive relationship between board diversity and earnings quality (Hoang et al. 2017), to name a few.

Overall, it is clear that there are a wide range of approaches in studying factors that are associated with firm performance in Vietnam. Most research articles in this area tend to focus on capital structure, board diversity, and ownership. Another striking issue is that measure of firm performance in Vietnam appears to vary greatly, which is also an issue for research studies around the world. For example, Vu et al. (2016) used Return on Assets (ROA), Swierczek and Ha (2003) used net profit, and Vo and Nguyen (2014) used four measures (ROA), return on equity (ROE), Z-score and Tobin's Q. It appears that firm performance measured using net income per employee has not been deployed in Vietnam. This paper will focus on this understudied area of the literature by analyzing the association between net income per employee and predictor variables such as firms' wage, competition, age, and CEO's sex. Analyzing pure cross-sectional data of 693 firms which are listed via the Ho Chi Minh City Stock

Exchange (HOSE) and Hanoi Stock Exchange (HNX) indices using both OLS and quantile regression methods, this study will triangulate the empirical results coming from analyzing the correlates of three indicators of firm performance: net income per employee, ROA, and ROE.

2. Materials and Methods

2.1. Data and Variables

This study started in 2016, at the time, 2015 was the latest year for which data on listed Vietnamese firms were published. Hence, data on these firms in 2015 were obtained from FiinPro (StoxPlus), which provides an extensive range of comprehensive financial information covering Vietnam's market, including around 800 listed firms and 1200 public unlisted firms. The database includes 693 firms operating in different sectors (Industry Division ICB 5), which include IT, industry, service consumption, petroleum, pharmaceuticals and health service, consumer goods, banking, materials, finance, and public utility sectors. All firms in our sample are listed on HNX and HOSE of Vietnam. The data were processed with Stata 14.0. Summary statistics of all variables used in the regression are provided in Table 1.

Table 1. Descriptive statistics of the dataset.

Variable Name	Variable Code	Mean	Standard Deviation	Min	Max	Observations
Dependent variable: Firm performance	"Firm performance"					
Net income per employee	"NIE"	21.1	1.23	14.06	25.51	639
ROA	"ROA"	0.064	0.081	−0.292	0.839	653
ROE	"ROE"	0.121	0.146053	−0.9993	1.4907	653
Explanatory variable:						
Competition	"COP"	0.12	0.42	0	0.74	693
Wage	"Wage"	0.1	0.1	0	2.49	672
Sex of CEO (dummy)	"Sex"	1.92	0.2	0	1	689
Age		5.75	3.02	0	15	693
Capital intensity	"CapIntensity"	0.36	0.66	0	6.84	672
Size Total number of employees	"Size" "SizeEmp"	27.2	1.64	23.28	34.37	690
International trade (dummy)	"InterTrade"	0.21	0.4	0	1	690

Regarding the dependent variable, this study follows the literature on measuring firm-level employee performance by dividing a firm's net income over its total number of employees, which takes the form of natural logarithm (Brandt et al. 2012; Choudhary 2014; Davis and Daley 2008; Sun and Yu 2015). This measure is sometimes referred to as a measure of firm-level productivity, which falls into the broader consideration of firm performance (Boardman et al. 2013; Davis and Daley 2008; Zhang and Xia 2013). Besides considering this unconventional indicator of firm performance, other conventional indicators, such as ROE and ROA, will also be examined.

For the explanatory variables, the Competition variable is constructed by dividing a firm's income over the total income of 693 firms in 2015. Competition variable varies from 0 to 0.74 with a mean value of 0.12 and standard deviation is 0.4. The wage of a firm measures the average labor cost over its total number of employees. In fact, wage per employee is a better measure because employees are heterogeneous factors across sectors. Characteristics of a firm's CEO, specifically the CEO's sex, is also taken into account. Studies such as Brennan and McCafferty (1997) suggest that female executives may have a better understanding of consumer behavior and customers' needs, which may create a competitive advantage for female-controlled firms. The age of a firm is the number of years since a firm was first listed. The capital intensity variable is measured by dividing the net fixed assets of a firm by its number of employees. This may also provide information on whether a firm is more labor-intensive or is more invested in technology. In this study, firm size is measured by the total number of employees.

2.2. Methods: OLS and Quantile Regression

The regression model follows the OLS method and takes the form of:

$$\begin{aligned} Firm\ performance_i &= \alpha_0 + \beta_1 Competition_i + \beta_2 Wage_i + \beta_3 Sex_i + \beta_4 Age_i \\ &+ \beta_5 CapIntesity_i + \beta_6 Size_i + \beta_7 InterTrade_i + \mu_i \end{aligned}$$

In the model, subscript i denotes firm i and μ_i is the error term (see Figure 1).

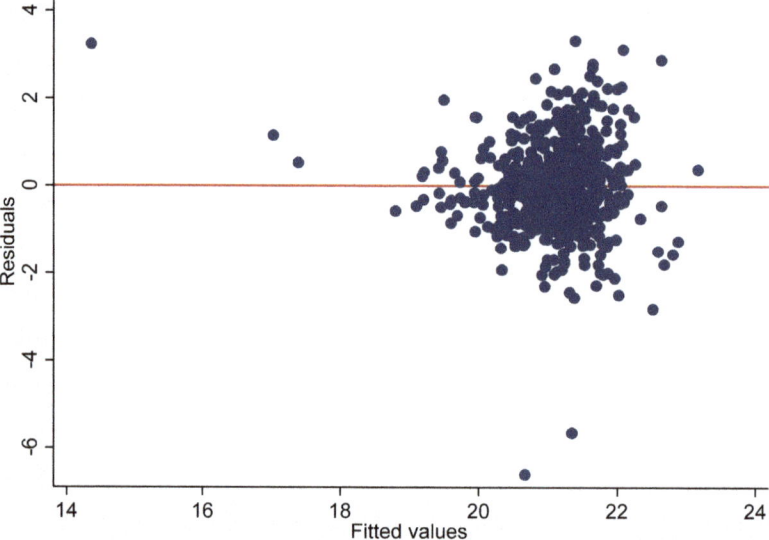

Figure 1. Firm performance varies across industries. The Y axis in the graph plots residuals obtained by regressing firm performance with variables in the right-hand side. The X axis plots firm performance (net income per employee).

Besides the OLS method, the quantile regression method has also been deployed. As the dataset contains a significant number of extreme values especially firms are heterogeneous in terms of capital commutation, the OLS method may not yield efficient estimators due to the linear model between a set of regressors and the outcome variable is based on the conditional mean function $E(y|x)$. We are therefore interested in obtaining regression coefficients for the relationship between the regressors and the dependent variable by using the conditional median function $Q_q(y|x)$. While estimators obtained from OLS based on minimizing the total sum of squared error $\left(\sum_i \varepsilon_i^2\right)$, the quantile regression method known as least-absolute-deviations (LAD) developed by Honoré (1992) minimizes $\sum_i |\varepsilon_i|$. More importantly, quantile regression is a better alternative method if the errors are highly non-normal. This method, providing a richer characterization of the data, allows us to entangle the impact of a covariate on the entire distribution of the response variable rather than its conditional mean (Baum 2013).

3. Results

3.1. Based Regression Results for the Correlates of Net Income per Employee

First, as endogeneity among the variables is a major obstacle in understanding the relationship among the variables in empirical studies on firm performance (Li 2016), this study tested the endogeneity problem by checking the correlation among the independent variables. The results of the correlation matrix are shown in Table 2 below, and it is notable that there is no strong correlation among all the independent variables.

Table 2. Correlation matrix of the independent variables.

	COP	Wage	Sex	Age	CapIntensity	SizeEmp
COP	1					
Wage	−0.0707	1				
Sex	−0.0658	0.0125	1			
Age	0.0375	0.1019 *	−0.0241	1		
CapIntensity	−0.0327	0.0203	0.0302	−0.0366	1	
SizeEmp	0.3419 *	−0.298 *	0.0508	0.0776 *	0.1517 *	1

* $p < 0.1$ (statistically significant at the conventional 10% level).

Next, the regression is performed for small and medium sized firms to evaluate how these two factors affect firms' performance differently. In general, the signs of all coefficients across models are consistent, although their magnitudes, in some cases, show considerable differences. It should be noted that all standard errors of coefficients have been adjusted for robustness. Firm's heterogeneity among sectors is also controlled for in the column S&M (stands for Small and Medium) of Table 3.

Table 3. Regression results for small and medium sized firms.

Variable	Small	Medium	S&M
"COP"	5.712 ***	0.362 ***	0.005
	(0.879)	(0.0787)	(0.63)
"Wage"	−2.479 ***	−4.359 ***	−2.69 ***
	(0.355)	(0.373)	(−10.65)
"Sex"	0.232	−0.125	−0.02
	(0.339)	(0.160)	(−0.15)
"Age"	−0.0892 ***	−0.0120	−0.05 ***
	(0.0276)	(0.0147)	(−3.35)
"CapIntensity"	−0.0878	−0.307 ***	−0.32 ***
	(0.0842)	(0.0967)	(−4.85)
"SizeEmp"			0.24 ***
			(7.10)
"InterTrade"	0.376	−0.0338	−0.10
	(0.258)	(0.0976)	(−0.85)
Constant	21.46 ***	21.74 ***	15.71 ***
	(0.664)	(0.337)	(0.941)
Observations	254	383	611
R-squared	0.33	0.34	0.30

Notes: *** significant at 1%. Absolute *t*-statistics are in parentheses.

In line with the existing literature, the higher the level of firms' competition, the higher their net income per employee denoting that when firms are able to gain more their market share, they are motivated to increase their productivity.

The wage cost of firms negatively affects the net income per employee of both small and medium sized firms with a 1% level of significance (β_2 equals −2.479 and −4.359 respectively, *p*-value < 0.01), implying that highly skilled workers are not actually needed in these low-technology firms. Theoretical and empirical studies have shown effect of a worker's wage on productivity depends on the country of origin. Specifically, a high wage per worker is more likely to encourage the labor productivity of developed countries, whereas it reduces the labor productivity of developing and less-developed countries (Kumar 1994; Papadogonas et al. 2007; Van Dijk 2002). A possible explanation is that low-cost labor remains a competitive advantage for these countries.

Firm age shows a negative and significant sign, indicating that younger firms tend to be more dynamic, thus finding it easier to adapt to changes in the law and business environment. Meanwhile, we found the sex of the CEO or chairperson to be insignificant. It has been found that for Vietnam, capital intensity has a negative association with the performance of listed firms implying that these low-tech and labor-intensive products do not require much capital.

We continue to examine whether the correlations of various factors with performance remain consistent if data sample is split based on financial and nonfinancial status. Although the magnitude of each coefficient changes slightly, the signs are consistent except for the competition (Table 4). The competition is no longer significant if we check the financial status as well as the international trade status of firms (Table 5).

Table 4. Regression results for financial and nonfinancial firms.

Variable	Financial (F)	Non-Financial (NF)
"COP"	−0.187	0.0761
	(0.524)	(0.104)
"Wage"	−1.593 ***	−4.252 ***
	(0.425)	(0.355)
"Sex"	−0.202	−0.0239
	(0.504)	(0.169)
"Age"	−0.140 **	−0.0438 ***
	(0.0654)	(0.0140)
"CapIntensity"	−0.288	−0.203 ***
	(0.195)	(0.0643)
"SizeEmp"	0.0904	0.231 ***
	(0.119)	(0.0346)
"InterTrade"	0.604	−0.167
	(0.582)	(0.102)
Constant	20.00 ***	15.73 ***
	(3.397)	(0.991)
Observations	84	553
R-squared	0.225	0.368

Notes: ** statistically significant at 5%; *** 1%. Absolute t-statistics are in parentheses. For both financial and nonfinancial firms, R-squared equals 0.086.

Table 5. Regression results for export-import firms.

Variable	International Trading Firms (IT)	Non-International Trading Firms (NIT)	Both (ITNIT)
"COP"	0.0411	0.119	0.0830
	(0.127)	(0.189)	(0.106)
"Wage"	−4.484 ***	−2.714 ***	−2.857 ***
	(0.866)	(0.271)	(0.258)
"Sex"	−0.227	0.242	0.00111
	(0.236)	(0.224)	(0.164)
"Age"	−0.0705 **	−0.0528 ***	−0.0586 ***
	(0.0277)	(0.0166)	(0.0142)
"CapIntensity"	−0.515 ***	−0.194 ***	−0.232 ***
	(0.191)	(0.0666)	(0.0625)

Table 5. Cont.

Variable	International Trading Firms (IT)	Non-International Trading Firms (NIT)	Both (ITNIT)
"SizeEmp"	0.267 ***	0.207 ***	0.226 ***
	(0.0698)	(0.0381)	(0.0324)
"InterTrade"			−0.0852
			(0.105)
Constant	15.25 ***	15.69 ***	15.71 ***
	(2.025)	(1.105)	(0.941)
Observations	137	500	637
R-squared	0.405	0.287	0.301

Notes: ** $p < 5\%$; *** $p < 1\%$. Absolute t-statistics are in parentheses.

3.2. Quantile Regression Results for Net Income per Employee

We compared different quantile models by regressing net income per employee with identified explanatory variables. We applied quantile regression for quantiles smaller and larger 50th whereby τ can be identified at 25th, 50th and 75th. Table 6 reports and compares regression results of OLS and five different quantile models for small and medium sized firms. Although the signs of Competition are mixed and insignificant for the total sample at all quantiles, they are consistently and significantly positive particularly for small firms indicating that a great market share occupation of firms in small size is necessarily important to enhance their firm performance. It is noteworthy that Competition shows no significant effect if a firm's financial and international statuses are controlled (Tables 7 and 8). An important point to note is that high-wage firms are not productive compared with the low ones.

At the 75th quantile, the role of a male CEO or Chairperson is significant for small firms when the size of firms is controlled even though its impact is not straightforward. The age of firm is consistently negative, confirming the empirical strand of literature that young firms are more dynamic and adapt better with market changes. For small firms, capital intensity is negative and significant only at the 25th quantile. Consistent with the OLS regression for firm size, firm size estimate effects at different quantiles are positive to firm performance implying that firms can increase productivity by expanding their economies of scale. The magnitude of firm size effect at median is lower than that of the OLS effect. From the 25th to 90th quantile, a firm's size does not change significantly; nonetheless, at 25th quantile, it is fairly small compared with the others and is significant at 1%.

Listed firms who are involved in international trade are considered to be more motivated to increase their productivity because in a broader and dynamic international market, firms need to increase productivity to exist. Literature on firms' export status and productivity confirms the causality relationship between firms' export status and their productivity and vice versa. Because the information on export status of firms is inexplicit, we created a dummy variable for firms who are involved in either export, import activities or in both export-import activities. The regression results show that only at 75th quantile for smaller firms, international trade status encourages labor productivity, whereas at the remaining quantiles, firms, international trade status has no relationship with firms' net income per employee.

Table 6. Quantile regression results by firms' size.

Variables	(0.25) Small 1	(0.50) Small 2	(0.75) Small 3	(0.25) Medium 4	(0.50) Medium 5	(0.75) Medium 6	(0.25) S&M 7	(0.50) S&M 8	(0.75) S&M 9
Competition	10.04 ***	8.764 *	6.614 **	0.215	0.506	0.970 ***	0.0368	-0.0503	0.230
	(3.789)	(4.527)	(2.662)	(0.280)	(0.395)	(0.372)	(0.0782)	(0.226)	(0.373)
Wage	-3.649 ***	-3.164 ***	-2.549 **	-4.401 ***	-4.905 ***	-5.384 ***	-3.899 ***	-4.253 ***	-3.459 ***
	(1.010)	(1.095)	(1.230)	(0.437)	(0.601)	(0.590)	(0.473)	(0.665)	(0.812)
Sex of CEO	0.270	0.0438	0.822 **	-0.406	-0.272	-0.171	-0.201	-0.0972	0.139
	(0.334)	(0.436)	(0.322)	(0.259)	(0.174)	(0.180)	(0.139)	(0.111)	(0.276)
Age	-0.0596 *	-0.0580 *	-0.104 ***	-0.00551	-0.0200	-0.0178	-0.0377 **	-0.0316 *	-0.0564 ***
	(0.0344)	(0.0328)	(0.0336)	(0.0193)	(0.0186)	(0.0108)	(0.0169)	(0.0167)	(0.0170)
Capital intensity	-0.0952	-0.00576	-0.110	-0.328 **	-0.151	-0.180	-0.151	-0.146	-0.223 **
	(0.172)	(0.118)	(0.0853)	(0.148)	(0.199)	(0.172)	(0.157)	(0.103)	(0.0879)
International trade	-0.0201	0.192	0.762 **	-0.189	-0.229 *	-0.135	-0.170 **	-0.223 **	-0.0977
	(0.385)	(0.374)	(0.371)	(0.122)	(0.127)	(0.140)	(0.0767)	(0.0877)	(0.187)
Financial firms	-0.297	0.110	0.136	-0.348	-0.322	-0.252	-0.327 **	-0.249	-0.0216
	(0.290)	(0.236)	(0.260)	(0.226)	(0.246)	(0.260)	(0.160)	(0.210)	(0.219)
Size							0.148 ***	0.192 ***	0.253 ***
							(0.0390)	(0.0412)	(0.0605)
Constant	20.71 ***	21.62 ***	21.01 ***	21.82 ***	22.11 ***	22.35 ***	17.66 ***	16.77 ***	15.31 ***
	(0.766)	(0.903)	(0.677)	(0.484)	(0.422)	(0.384)	(1.081)	(1.133)	(1.398)
Observations	254	254	254	383	383	383	637	637	637

Notes: * statistically significant at 10%; ** 5%; *** 1%. Absolute of t-statistics of OLS regression are in parentheses. Coefficients and standard errors of quantile regressions are bootstrapped. Bootstrap is performed with 20 replications.

Table 7. Quantile regression results for financial (F) and nonfinancial firms (NF).

Variables	(0.25) F	(0.50) F	(0.75) F	(0.25) NF	(0.50) NF	(0.75) NF	(0.25) FNF	(0.50) FNF	(0.75) FNF
Competition	−0.0294	−0.393	−0.187	0.0369	0.173	0.264	0.0368	−0.0503	0.230
	(1.987)	(2.378)	(4.247)	(0.228)	(0.282)	(0.386)	(0.105)	(0.137)	(0.347)
Wage	−1.489 ***	−1.482 *	−1.827	−4.238 ***	−5.203 ***	−4.885 ***	−3.899 ***	−4.253 ***	−3.459 ***
	(0.498)	(0.881)	(1.189)	(0.536)	(0.467)	(0.512)	(0.451)	(0.905)	(1.181)
Sex of CEO	−0.148	−0.384	0.0899	−0.275	−0.0649	0.00667	−0.201	−0.0972	0.139
	(0.444)	(0.528)	(0.605)	(0.168)	(0.154)	(0.222)	(0.209)	(0.140)	(0.189)
Age	−0.0476	−0.0427	−0.209 **	−0.0369 *	−0.0253 **	−0.0358 *	−0.0377 ***	−0.0316 ***	−0.0564 **
	(0.0779)	(0.112)	(0.0986)	(0.0212)	(0.0121)	(0.0196)	(0.0139)	(0.0122)	(0.0219)
Capital intensity	−0.0519	−0.362 **	−0.464	−0.149	−0.0759	−0.143	−0.151	−0.146	−0.223 **
	(0.174)	(0.142)	(0.347)	(0.150)	(0.0552)	(0.0891)	(0.149)	(0.104)	(0.0969)
International trade	0.105	0.124	0.0481	0.150 ***	0.172 ***	0.250 ***	0.148 ***	0.192 ***	0.253 ***
	(0.184)	(0.176)	(0.178)	(0.0313)	(0.0291)	(0.0522)	(0.0303)	(0.0373)	(0.0552)
Financial firms	0.372	0.0399	1.642	−0.188 **	−0.209 ***	−0.281 *	−0.170 *	−0.223 **	−0.0977
	(0.754)	(1.140)	(1.108)	(0.0905)	(0.0768)	(0.161)	(0.0911)	(0.0894)	(0.155)
Size							−0.327 *	−0.249	−0.0216
							(0.173)	(0.188)	(0.229)
Constant	18.19 ***	19.00 ***	21.82 ***	17.78 ***	17.24 ***	15.66 ***	17.66 ***	16.77 ***	15.31 ***
	(4.934)	(5.127)	(5.436)	(0.906)	(0.921)	(1.489)	(1.013)	(1.168)	(1.624)
Observations	84	84	84	553	553	553	637	637	637

Notes: * statistically significant at 10%; ** 5%; *** 1%. Absolute of t-statistics of OLS regression are in parentheses. Coefficients and standard errors of quantile regressions are bootstrapped. Bootstrap is performed with 20 replications.

Table 8. Quantile regression results for noninternational trading firms.

Variables	(0.25) IT	(0.50) IT	(0.75) IT	(0.25) NIT	(0.50) NIT	(0.75) NIT	(0.25) ITNIT	(0.50) ITNIT	(0.75) ITNIT
Competition	0.0392 (0.494)	0.0742 (0.608)	0.128 (0.465)	0.0446 (0.0985)	−0.216 * (0.119)	−0.143 (0.643)	0.0368 (0.178)	−0.0503 (0.244)	0.230 (0.320)
Wage	−4.232 *** (1.016)	−5.559 *** (1.577)	−4.915 ** (1.907)	−3.585 *** (0.570)	−3.903 *** (0.747)	−3.483 *** (1.104)	−3.899 *** (0.424)	−4.253 *** (0.655)	−3.459 *** (0.873)
Sex of CEO	−0.348 (0.367)	−0.323 (0.379)	−0.392 (0.250)	0.0321 (0.210)	0.134 (0.159)	0.514 * (0.305)	−0.201 (0.153)	−0.0972 (0.130)	0.139 (0.242)
Age	−0.0527 (0.0351)	−0.0496 (0.0371)	−0.0743 ** (0.0363)	−0.0324 (0.0201)	−0.0176 (0.0161)	−0.0569 *** (0.0215)	−0.0377 *** (0.0114)	−0.0316 *** (0.0118)	−0.0564 ** (0.0219)
Capital intensity	−0.752 ** (0.361)	−0.179 (0.420)	−0.149 (0.320)	−0.119 (0.0877)	−0.169 ** (0.0815)	−0.223 * (0.115)	−0.151 (0.141)	−0.146 * (0.0878)	−0.223 ** (0.0907)
International trade	0.122 (0.123)	0.226 * (0.119)	0.325 ** (0.140)	0.143 *** (0.0510)	0.208 *** (0.0418)	0.211 *** (0.0591)	0.148 *** (0.0333)	0.192 *** (0.0410)	0.253 *** (0.0430)
Financial firms	−0.235 (1.126)	0.150 (1.222)	1.276 (1.334)	−0.337 * (0.183)	−0.256 (0.207)	−0.0433 (0.138)	−0.327 ** (0.148)	−0.249 (0.168)	−0.0216 (0.224)
Size							−0.170 ** (0.0685)	−0.223 ** (0.0977)	−0.0977 (0.153)
Constant	18.79 *** (3.370)	16.35 *** (3.320)	14.38 *** (3.781)	17.25 *** (1.393)	15.79 *** (1.177)	15.76 *** (1.728)	17.66 *** (0.726)	16.77 *** (1.196)	15.31 *** (1.305)
Observations	137	137	137	500	500	500	637	637	637

Notes: * statistically significant at 10%; ** 5%; *** 1%. Absolute of t-statistics of OLS regression are in parentheses. Coefficients and standard errors of quantile regressions are bootstrapped. Bootstrap is performed with 20 replications.

3.3. ROA and ROE as Firm Performance Measures

The regression results for the net income per employee as a measure of firm performance has pointed out the negative association of the dependent variable with factors such as wage, age, and capital intensity. Comparing the regression results for ROA and ROE as measures of firm performance can help put these results in a broader perspective. Table 9 shows the results for the correlates of ROA for small and medium firms. The major results for ROE are summarized in the main text and the full details can be found in Appendix A.

Similar to the results for net income per employee, the OLS regression for ROA and ROE shows that capital intensity (measured by net assets divided by the number of employees) is negatively associated with firm performance ($\beta_5 = -0.00621$; p-value < 0.1).

We also find that for financial firms, age and wage are negatively correlated with ROA similar to the results for net income per employee (Table 10). This is a similar pattern for net income per employee (Table 3) and ROE (the Appendix A).

Table 9. Correlates of ROA for small and medium firms.

Variable	Small	Medium	S&M
"COP"	−0.00132 ***	0.000701	0.000993 *
	(0.000368)	(0.000453)	(0.000522)
"Wage"	−0.0361	0.0276	−0.0184
	(0.0219)	(0.0306)	(0.0164)
"Sex"	0.00416	−0.0119	−0.00977
	(0.0187)	(0.0163)	(0.0139)
"Age"	0.000352	−0.00246	−0.00136
	(0.00233)	(0.00159)	(0.00126)
"CapIntensity"	−0.0107 *	−0.00774	−0.00621 *
	(0.00546)	(0.00503)	(0.00369)
"InterTrade"	−0.0235	0.00567	0.00487
	(0.0181)	(0.00779)	(0.00750)
"SizeEmp"			−0.00480 *
			(0.00258)
Constant	0.0645 ***	0.0906 ***	0.214 ***
	(0.0188)	(0.0196)	(0.0728)
Observations	133	471	604
R-squared	0.026	0.015	0.015

Notes: * statistically significant at 10%; *** 1%. Absolute t-statistics are in parentheses.

Table 10. Correlates of ROA for financial and nonfinancial firms.

Variable	Financial (F)	Non-Financial (NF)	Both (FNF)
"COP"	6.49×10^{-5}	0.000931 *	0.000760
	(0.000671)	(0.000562)	(0.000510)
"Wage"	−0.0122 **	−0.0270	−0.0182
	(0.00580)	(0.0325)	(0.0168)
"Sex"	0.0172	−0.0190	−0.0122
	(0.0116)	(0.0166)	(0.0136)
"Age"	−0.00628 ***	−0.00155	−0.00186
	(0.00206)	(0.00138)	(0.00127)
"CapIntensity"	−0.0214 **	−0.00425	−0.00734 **
	(0.00965)	(0.00425)	(0.00366)
"InterTrade"	0.00742	-1.57×10^{-6}	0.000697
	(0.0149)	(0.00827)	(0.00788)
"SizeEmp"	0.00424	−0.00374	−0.00267
	(0.00454)	(0.00329)	(0.00282)
"Finance"			−0.0299 ***
			(0.00769)
Constant	−0.0551	0.200 **	0.167 **
	(0.122)	(0.0910)	(0.0768)
Observations	82	522	604
R-squared	0.188	0.013	0.028

Notes: * statistically significant at 10%; ** 5%; *** 1%. Absolute t-statistics are in parentheses.

For a firm who engages in international trade, only competition has a significant positive correlation with ROA (Table 11) and ROE (the Appendix A). This result stands in contrary to when we regress competition with net income over employee.

Table 11. Correlates of ROA for international trading firms and noninternational-trading firms.

Variable	International Trading Firms (IT)	Noninternational Trading Firms (NIT)	Both (ITNIT)
"COP"	0.00160 **	0.000521	0.000993 *
	(0.000786)	(0.000804)	(0.000522)
"Wage"	0.0500	−0.0255	−0.0184
	(0.0837)	(0.0170)	(0.0164)
"Sex"	−0.0341	0.00227	−0.00977
	(0.0227)	(0.0169)	(0.0139)
"Age"	0.000136	−0.00196	−0.00136
	(0.00161)	(0.00158)	(0.00126)
"CapIntensity"	−0.000912	−0.00669 *	−0.00621 *
	(0.0117)	(0.00392)	(0.00369)
"SizeEmp"	−0.00803	−0.00406	−0.00480 *
	(0.00562)	(0.00293)	(0.00258)
"InterTrade"			0.00487
			(0.00750)
Constant	0.309 *	0.188 **	0.214 ***
	(0.159)	(0.0825)	(0.0728)
Observations	127	477	604
R-squared	0.070	0.014	0.015

Notes: * statistically significant at 10%; ** 5%; *** 1%. Absolute t-statistics are in parentheses.

4. Discussion

4.1. Limitations and Recommendations

This study has several limitations. First, the study only looks at three dimensions of firm performance, namely, net income per employee, ROA and ROE. That means future studies can look at other more traditional indicators of firm performances, such as earning per share (EPS), percentage of sales from new products (Davis and Daley 2008; Vu et al. 2016), earning quality (Hoang et al. 2017), and Tobin's Q (Vu et al. 2016). Second, as this study only investigates the year 2015, it is imperative to expand the study to collect data from other years. Cross-sectional time series data would provide a more comprehensive understanding of the issue and an extension of the technical as well as theoretical contribution. For example, it is possible to probe the effectiveness of different methods in treating the endogeneity problem with the panel data (Li 2016).

In addition, this study only samples public firms; thus, it remains uncertain whether these conclusions hold for private firms. Moreover, since there are many different proxies to firm size, one can compare and contrast the empirical results when using other indicators such as total assets or total revenues. As Dang et al. (2018) have pointed out, analyses can be sensitive for different measures of firm size. Regarding the variable the sex of CEO, future studies can expand on this issue by constructing this variable differently, for example, whether a company has women on their board of directors (Carter et al. 2003; Krishnan and Park 2005; Rose 2007). As firm performance can also be influenced by various cultural factors, it is necessary for future studies to expand in this direction (Vuong et al. 2018; Vuong 2016b).

We have been particularly interested in identifying the association of competition, wage, and firm performance in Vietnam's listed firms; about 13% of the firms are operating in the financial sector and about 20% of the firms are doing international trade. Although the OLS approach enables us to examine the effects of firms' wage and competition on their performance, the quantiles regression method is also used because it yields richer characterization of the data. In this respect, we observe that firms are highly heterogeneous within a single sector. The regression results of OLS and quantiles approach show that almost all the mean and median estimates of independent variables are very different, except for firms' capital intensity, thus confirming our concern about the heterogeneity of firms. The magnitude of firms' capital intensity varies largely when firms' size and financial status is controlled for. Studying the correlates of firm performance is an important area for both business and government; thus, this under-researched area in Vietnam should be investigated further to prevent failures of policy and business strategy (Vuong 2018).

4.2. Implications

First of all, whether firm performance is measured by net income per employee, ROA, or ROE, this study consistently confirms that the sex of the CEO or chairperson is not significant in explaining firm performance. Moreover, there is a negative association between capital intensity and firm performance. As for financial firms, the age of a firm and average wage per employee are negatively associated with all types of performance indicators. When viewing all the pieces of evidence together, this study points to the fact that Vietnam's business activities are still concentrating on low labor cost, labor intensive, and low-tech production.

Considering that studies have shown that relying too much on abundant resources will be a curse as it hinders firms' ability to innovate (Vuong 2016a) and women directors having crucial role in companies where innovation is a strategic focus (Dezsö and Ross 2012), one realizes that although low cost of labor may be regarded as a competitive advantage of many sectors of Vietnam, in the age of Industry 4.0, overdependence on this factor can hamper firms' ability to adapt and thrive. Furthermore, in order for Vietnam to achieve a higher position in the global value chain and compete better in the international market, policy makers need to promote high-tech industries, which in turn encourage more highly skilled and better-paid workers.

Author Contributions: Conceptualization, T.-H.V.; methodology, T.-H.V.; software, V.-D.N.; validation, M.-T.H. and Q.-H.V.; formal analysis, T.-H.V.; investigation, V.-D.N.; resources, Q.-H.V.; data curation, V.-D.N.; writing—original draft preparation, T.-H.V.; writing—review and editing, M.-T.H.; visualization, V.-D.N.; supervision, Q.-H.V.; project administration, Q.-H.V.

Funding: This research received no external funding.

Conflicts of Interest: The authors declare no conflict of interest.

Appendix A

Table A1. Correlates of ROE for small and medium firms.

Variable	Small	Medium	S&M
"COP"	0.000752	0.00183 *	0.00154
	(0.000691)	(0.000941)	(0.000941)
"Wage"	−0.0567	0.0175	−0.0219
	(0.0417)	(0.0641)	(0.0335)
"Sex"	−0.000912	0.00145	0.00231
	(0.0346)	(0.0280)	(0.0238)
"Age"	−0.000208	−0.00460 **	−0.00268
	(0.00317)	(0.00226)	(0.00177)
"CapIntensity"	−0.0106	−0.0188 *	−0.0163 **
	(0.0102)	(0.0108)	(0.00735)
"InterTrade"	−0.0268	0.00264	0.00117
	(0.0299)	(0.0144)	(0.0134)
"SizeEmp"			0.00337
			(0.00399)
Constant	0.106 ***	0.159 ***	0.0500
	(0.0342)	(0.0342)	(0.114)
Observations	133	471	604
R-squared	0.013	0.017	0.013

Notes: * significant at 10%; ** 5%; *** 1%. Absolute *t*-statistics are in parentheses.

Table A2. Correlates of ROE for financial and nonfinancial firms.

Variable	Financial (F)	Nonfinancial (NF)	Both (FNF)
"COP"	−0.00112	0.00137	0.00105
	(0.00125)	(0.000973)	(0.000900)
"Wage"	−0.0162 *	−0.0281	−0.0214
	(0.00937)	(0.0647)	(0.0323)
"Sex"	0.0351 *	−0.0132	−0.00266
	(0.0203)	(0.0283)	(0.0232)
"Age"	−0.00849 **	−0.00340 *	−0.00374 **
	(0.00337)	(0.00195)	(0.00180)
"CapIntensity"	−0.0308 **	−0.0160 *	−0.0187 **
	(0.0142)	(0.00827)	(0.00726)
"InterTrade"	−0.00794	−0.00835	−0.00749
	(0.0365)	(0.0146)	(0.0139)
"SizeEmp"	0.0177 *	0.00656	0.00779 *
	(0.00935)	(0.00482)	(0.00424)
"Finance"			−0.0620 ***
			(0.0137)
Constant	−0.389	−0.00684	−0.0472
	(0.250)	(0.136)	(0.117)
Observations	82	522	604
R-squared	0.124	0.017	0.031

Notes: * significant at 10%; ** 5%; *** 1%. Absolute t-statistics are in parentheses.

Table A3. Correlates of ROE for international trading firms and non-international-trading firms.

Variable	International Trading Firms (IT)	Noninternational Trading Firms (NIT)	Both (ITNIT)
"COP"	0.00189 **	0.00170	0.00154
	(0.000768)	(0.00187)	(0.000940)
"Wage"	0.00738	−0.0239	−0.0219
	(0.167)	(0.0335)	(0.0335)
"Sex"	−0.0185	0.0103	0.00210
	(0.0353)	(0.0322)	(0.0236)
"Age"	−0.00123	−0.00317	−0.00265
	(0.00307)	(0.00215)	(0.00177)
"CapIntensity"	−0.00145	−0.0176 **	−0.0164 **
	(0.0282)	(0.00762)	(0.00729)
"SizeEmp"	−0.00526	0.00487	0.00341
	(0.00934)	(0.00453)	(0.00396)
"InterTrade"	0.289	0.00530	0.0491
	(0.266)	(0.128)	(0.113)
Constant	127	477	604
	0.017	0.015	0.013
Observations	0.00189 **	0.00170	0.00154
R-squared	(0.000768)	(0.00187)	(0.000940)

Notes: ** significant at 5%; Absolute t-statistics are in parentheses.

References

Andersson, Martin, Sara Johansson, and Hans Lööf. 2012. Firm performance and international trade–evidence from a small open economy. In *The Regional Economics of Knowledge and Talent: Local Advantage in a Global Context*. Edited by Charlie Karlsson, Borje Johanson and Roger. R. Stough. Glos: Edward Elgar Publishing, pp. 320–42.

Baum, C. 2013. Quantile Regression, Lecture Notes for Applied Econometrics. Available online: http://fmwww.bc.edu/EC-C/S2013/823/EC823.S2013.nn04.slides.pdf (accessed on 17 March 2019).

Boardman, Anthony E., Claude Laurin, Mark A. Moore, and Aidan R. Vining. 2013. Efficiency, profitability and welfare gains from the Canadian National Railway privatization. *Research in Transportation Business & Management* 6: 19–30.

Bourlès, Renaud, Gilbert Cette, Jimmy Lopez, Jacques Mairesse, and Giuseppe Nicoletti. 2013. Do product market regulations in upstream sectors curb productivity growth? Panel data evidence for OECD countries. *Review of Economics and Statistics* 95: 1750–68. [CrossRef]

Brandt, Loren, Johannes Van Biesebroeck, and Yifan Zhang. 2012. Creative accounting or creative destruction? Firm-level productivity growth in Chinese manufacturing. *Journal of Development Economics* 97: 339–51. [CrossRef]

Brennan, Niamh M., and Jacqueline McCafferty. 1997. Corporate governance practices in Irish companies. *IBAR–Irish Business and Administrative Research* 18: 116–35.

Camisón, César, and Ana Villar-López. 2014. Organizational innovation as an enabler of technological innovation capabilities and firm performance. *Journal of Business Research* 67: 2891–902. [CrossRef]

Carter, David A., Betty J. Simkins, and W. Gary Simpson. 2003. Corporate Governance, Board Diversity, and Firm Value. *Financial Review* 38: 33–53. [CrossRef]

Choudhary, Amod. 2014. Smartphones and their impact on net income per employee for selected U.S. firms. *Review of Business & Finance Studies* 5: 6–17.

Coles, Jeffrey L., Zhichuan Li, and Albert Y. Wang. 2017. Industry tournament incentives. *The Review of Financial Studies* 31: 1418–59. [CrossRef]

Core, John, and Wayne Guay. 1999. The use of equity grants to manage optimal equity incentive levels. *Journal of Accounting and Economics* 28: 151–84. [CrossRef]

Dang, Chongyu, Zhichuan Frank Li, and Chen Yang. 2018. Measuring firm size in empirical corporate finance. *Journal of Banking & Finance* 86: 159–76.

Davis, Deborah, and Barbara J. Daley. 2008. The learning organization and its dimensions as key factors in firms' performance. *Human Resource Development International* 11: 51–66. [CrossRef]

De Loecker, Jan, and Jan Van Biesebroeck. 2018. Effect of international competition on firm productivity and market power. In *The Oxford Handbook of Productivity Analysis*. Edited by Emili Grifell-Tatjé, Knox C. A. Lovell and Robin C. Sickles. New York: Oxford University Press, p. 463.

Dezsö, Cristian L., and David Gaddis Ross. 2012. Does female representation in top management improve firm performance? A panel data investigation. *Strategic Management Journal* 33: 1072–89. [CrossRef]

Doğan, Mesut. 2013. Does firm size affect the firm profitability? Evidence from Turkey. *Research Journal of Finance and Accounting* 4: 53–59.

Garicano, Luis, Claire Lelarge, and John Van Reenen. 2016. Firm size distortions and the productivity distribution: Evidence from france. *American Economic Review* 106: 3439–79. [CrossRef]

Garicano, Luis, Claire Lelarge, and John Van Reenen. 2017. *Size-Based Regulations and Firm Growth: Is Small Beautiful?* Paris: Rue de la Banque, Banque de France.

GERA. 2018. *Global Entrepreneurship Monitor 2017/2018 Global Report*. Babson Park: Global Entrepreneurship Research Association, Available online: https://www.gemconsortium.org/report/50012 (accessed on 11 April 2019).

Giroud, Xavier, and Holger M. Mueller. 2011. Corporate governance, product market competition, and equity prices. *The Journal of Finance* 66: 563–600. [CrossRef]

Hoang, Trang Cam, Indra Abeysekera, and Shiguang Ma. 2017. The effect of board diversity on earnings quality: An empirical study of listed firms in Vietnam. *Australian Accounting Review* 27: 146–63. [CrossRef]

Honoré, Bo E. 1992. Trimmed LAD and least squares estimation of truncated and censored regression models with fixed effects. *Econometrica* 60: 533–65. [CrossRef]

Kopf, Dan. 2018. Vietnam Is the Most Globalized Populous Country in Modern History. Available online: https://www.weforum.org/agenda/2018/10/vietnam-is-the-most-globalized-populous-country-in-modern-history/ (accessed on 17 March 2019).

Krishnan, Hema A., and Daewoo Park. 2005. A few good women: On top management teams. *Journal of Business Research* 58: 1712–20. [CrossRef]

Kumar, Nagesh. 1994. Determinants of export orientation of foreign production by US multinationals: An inter-country analysis. *Journal of International Business Studies* 25: 141–56. [CrossRef]

Kurshev, Alexander, and Ilya A. Strebulaev. 2015. Firm size and capital structure. *Quarterly Journal of Finance* 5: 1550008. [CrossRef]

Le, Thi Phuong Vy, and Thi Bich Nguyet Phan. 2017. Capital structure and firm performance: Empirical evidence from a small transition country. *Research in International Business and Finance* 42: 710–26. [CrossRef]

Li, Zhichuan Frank. 2014. Mutual monitoring and corporate governance. *Journal of Banking & Finance* 45: 255–69.

Li, Zhichuan Frank. 2016. Endogeneity in CEO power: A survey and experiment. *Investment Analysts Journal* 45: 149–62. [CrossRef]

Liu, Yu, Zuobao Wei, and Feixue Xie. 2014. Do women directors improve firm performance in China? *Journal of Corporate Finance* 28: 169–84. [CrossRef]

Lückerath-Rovers, Mijntje. 2013. Women on boards and firm performance. *Journal of Management & Governance* 17: 491–509.

Munch, Jakob, and Georg Schaur. 2018. The effect of export promotion on firm-level performance. *American Economic Journal: Economic Policy* 10: 357–87. [CrossRef]

Nguyen, Bich Thi Ngoc, Hai Thi Thanh Tran, Oanh Hoang Le, Phuoc Thi Nguyen, Thien Hiep Trinh, and Viet Le. 2015. Association between corporate social responsibility disclosures and firm value–Empirical evidence from Vietnam. *International Journal of Accounting and Financial Reporting* 5: 212–28. [CrossRef]

Nhan Dan. 2017. Enhancing Role of Vietnamese Entrepreneurs in New Stage of Development. Available online: http://en.nhandan.org.vn/business/item/5566302-enhancing-role-of-vietnamese-entrepreneurs-in-new-stage-of-development.html (accessed on 14 February 2019).

Nickell, Stephen J. 1996. Competition and corporate performance. *Journal of Political Economy* 104: 724–46. [CrossRef]

Orlitzky, Marc. 2001. Does Firm Size Comfound the Relationship Between Corporate Social Performance and Firm Financial Performance? *Journal of Business Ethics* 33: 167–80. [CrossRef]

Schiffbauer, Marc, and Sandra Ospina. 2006. *Competition and Firm Productivity: Evidence from Firm-Level Data*. IMF Working Paper. Washington: International Monetary Fund.

Papadogonas, Theodore, Fotini Voulgaris, and George Agiomirgianakis. 2007. Determinants of export behavior in the Greek manufacturing sector. *Operational Research* 7: 121–35. [CrossRef]

Pham, Minh Chinh, and Quan Hoang Vuong. 2009. *Kinh te Vietnam: Thang tram va Dot Pha [Vietnam's Economy: Vissicitude and Breakthrough]*. Hanoi: NXB Tri thuc.

Phung, Duc Nam, and Thi Phuong Thao Hoang. 2013. Corporate ownership and firm performance in emerging market: A study of Vietnamese listed firms. Paper presented at World Business and Social Science Research Conference, Bangkok, Thailand, December 18–19.

Phung, Duc Nam, and Thi Phuong Vy Le. 2013. Foreign Ownership, Capital Structure and Firm Performance: Empirical Evidence from Vietnamese Listed Firms. *The IUP Journal of Corporate Governance* 12: 40–58.

Phung, Duc Nam, and Anil V. Mishra. 2016. Ownership structure and firm performance: Evidence from Vietnamese listed firms. *Australian Economic Papers* 55: 63–98. [CrossRef]

Piget, Patrick, and Mohamed Kossaï. 2013. The Relationship between Information and Communication Technology Use and Firm Performance in Developing Countries: A Case Study of Electrical and Electronic Goods Manufacturing SMEs in Tunisia. *African Development Review* 25: 330–43. [CrossRef]

Rose, Caspar. 2007. Does female board representation influence firm performance? The Danish evidence. *Corporate Governance: An International Review* 15: 404–13. [CrossRef]

Schreck, Philipp, and Sascha Raithel. 2015. Corporate social performance, firm size, and organizational visibility: Distinct and joint effects on voluntary sustainability reporting. *Business & Society* 57: 742–78.

Silva, Armando, Oscar Afonso, and Ana Paula Africano. 2013. Economic performance and international trade engagement: the case of Portuguese manufacturing firms. *International Economics and Economic Policy* 10: 521–47. [CrossRef]

Sun, Li, and T. Robert Yu. 2015. The impact of corporate social responsibility on employee performance and cost. *Review of Accounting and Finance* 14: 262–84. [CrossRef]

Swierczek, Fredric William, and Thai Thanh Ha. 2003. Entrepreneurial Orientation, Uncertainty Avoidance and Firm Performance: An Analysis of Thai and Vietnamese SMEs. *The International Journal of Entrepreneurship and Innovation* 4: 46–58. [CrossRef]

Tran, Ngo My, Walter Nonneman, and Ann Jorissen. 2014. Government ownership and firm performance: The case of Vietnam. *International Journal of Economics and Financial Issues* 4: 628–50.

Truong, Dong Loc, Ger Lanjouw, and Robert Lensink. 2006. The impact of privatization on firm performance in a transition economy: The case of Vietnam. *Economics of Transition* 14: 349–89.

Van Dijk, Michiel. 2002. *The Determinants of Export Performance in Developing Countries: The Case of Indonesian Manufacturing*. Eindhoven: Eindhoven Centre for Innovation Studies.

Vo, Duc Hong, and Tri Minh Nguyen. 2014. The impact of corporate governance on firm performance: Empirical study in Vietnam. *International Journal of Economics and Finance* 6: 1–13. [CrossRef]

Thanh, Vu Huu, and Nguyen Minh Ha. 2013. The effect of banking relationship on firm performance in Vietnam. *International Journal of Economics and Finance* 5: 148–58. [CrossRef]

Vu, Van Huong, Quang Tuyen Tran, Van Tuan Nguyen, and Steven Lim. 2016. Corruption, types of corruption and firm financial performance: New evidence from a transitional economy. *Journal of Business Ethics* 148: 847–58.

Vuong, Quan-Hoang. 2016a. Determinants of firm performance in a less innovative transition system: exploring Vietnamese longitudinal data. *International Journal of Transitions and Innovation Systems* 5: 20–45. [CrossRef]

Vuong, Quan-Hoang. 2016b. Impacts of geographical locations and sociocultural traits on the Vietnamese entrepreneurship. *SpringerPlus* 5: 1189. [CrossRef]

Vuong, Quan-Hoang. 2018. The (ir)rational consideration of the cost of science in transition economies. *Nature Human Behaviour* 2: 5. [CrossRef]

Vuong, Quan-Hoang. 2019a. Computational entrepreneurship: From economic complexities to interdisciplinary research. *Problems and Perspectives in Management* 17: 117–29. [CrossRef]

Vuong, Quan-Hoang. 2019b. The financial economy of Viet Nam in an age of reform, 1986–2016. In *Routledge Handbook of Banking and Finance in Asia*. Edited by Ulrich Volz, Peter J. Morgan and Naoyuki Yoshino. London: Routledge (T&F), pp. 201–22.

Vuong, Quan Hoang, and Tri Dung Tran. 2009. The cultural dimensions of the Vietnamese private entrepreneurship. *IUP Journal of Entrepreneurship Development* VI: 54–78. [CrossRef]

Vuong, Quan-Hoang, Quang-Khiem Bui, Viet-Phuong La, Thu-Trang Vuong, Viet-Ha T. Nguyen, Manh-Toan Ho, Hong-Kong T. Nguyen, and Manh-Tung Ho. 2018. Cultural additivity: behavioural insights from the interaction of Confucianism, Buddhism and Taoism in folktales. *Palgrave Communications* 4: 143. [CrossRef]

Vuong, Quan-Hoang, Manh-Tung Ho, Thu-Trang Vuong, Viet-Phuong La, Manh-Toan Ho, Kien-Cuong P. Nghiem, Bach Xuan Tran, Hai-Ha Giang, Thu-Vu Giang, Carl Latkin, and et al. 2019. Artificial Intelligence vs. Natural Stupidity: Evaluating AI Readiness for the Vietnamese Medical Information System. *Journal of Clinical Medicine* 8: 168. [CrossRef]

Wagner, Joachim. 2012. International trade and firm performance: A survey of empirical studies since 2006. *Review of World Economics* 148: 235–67. [CrossRef]

Wang, Zhining, and Nianxin Wang. 2012. Knowledge sharing, innovation and firm performance. *Expert Systems with Applications* 39: 8899–908. [CrossRef]

Wolff, James A., and Timothy L. Pett. 2000. Internationalization of small firms: An examination of export competitive patterns, firm size, and export performance. *Journal of Small Business Management* 38: 34.

Zhang, Guoqiang Peter, and Yusen Xia. 2013. Does quality still pay? A reexamination of the relationship between effective quality management and firm performance. *Production and Operations Management* 22: 120–36. [CrossRef]

© 2019 by the authors. Licensee MDPI, Basel, Switzerland. This article is an open access article distributed under the terms and conditions of the Creative Commons Attribution (CC BY) license (http://creativecommons.org/licenses/by/4.0/).

MDPI
St. Alban-Anlage 66
4052 Basel
Switzerland
Tel. +41 61 683 77 34
Fax +41 61 302 89 18
www.mdpi.com

Journal of Risk and Financial Management Editorial Office
E-mail: jrfm@mdpi.com
www.mdpi.com/journal/jrfm

www.ingramcontent.com/pod-product-compliance
Lightning Source LLC
LaVergne TN
LVHW070546100526
838202LV00012B/400